ALL THE WAY IN

Ecology and Justice

An Orbis Series on Integral Ecology

Advisory Board Members
Mary Evelyn Tucker
John A. Grim
Leonardo Boff
Sean McDonagh

ALL THE WAY IN

*A Story of Activism, Incarceration,
and Organic Farming*

by

JEANNE CLARK, OP

ORBIS BOOKS

Maryknoll, New York 10545

ORBIS BOOKS
Maryknoll, New York 10545

Fathers and Brothers
MARYKNOLL™

Founded in 1970, Orbis Books endeavors to publish works that enlighten the mind, nourish the spirit, and challenge the conscience. The publishing arm of the Maryknoll Fathers and Brothers, Orbis seeks to explore the global dimensions of the Christian faith and mission, to invite dialogue with diverse cultures and religious traditions, and to serve the cause of reconciliation and peace. The books published reflect the views of their authors and do not represent the official position of the Maryknoll Society. To learn more about Maryknoll and Orbis Books, please visit our website at www.maryknollsociety.org.

Library of Congress Cataloging-in-Publication Data

Names: Clark, Jeanne, 1938- author.
Title: All the way in : a story of activism, incarceration, and organic farming / Sr. Jeanne Clark, OP.
Description: Maryknoll, NY : Orbis Books, [2023] | Series: Ecology & justice | Includes bibliographical references and index. | Summary: "A memoir of Sister Jeanne Clark, a Dominican nun, whose call to follow the gospel-to go "all the way in"-led her on a journey through peacemaking, solidarity with refugees, and ultimately to her commitment to organic farming as a way of promoting earth-consciousness"— Provided by publisher.
Identifiers: LCCN 2022034933 (print) | LCCN 2022034934 (ebook) | ISBN 9781626985056 (trade paperback) | ISBN 9781608339679 (epub)
Subjects: LCSH: Clark, Jeanne, 1938- | Nuns—Biography. | Dominicans—Biography.
Classification: LCC BX4705.C5525 A3 2023 (print) | LCC BX4705.C5525 (ebook) | DDC 271/.9002 [B]—dc23/eng/20220906
LC record available at https://lccn.loc.gov/2022034933
LC ebook record available at https://lccn.loc.gov/2022034934

For the children and the young
of every species

Contents

Introduction

This book is about a journey . . . the journey home to the true self. We all are invited to take it, but each one is unique, filled with different places and people. I know for certain that all of our journeys that seem separate are each strands in a web of connection—a beautiful tapestry. We journey together, and each one of our lives contributes something that no other life can.

This book is about my story, my journey, but I hope that it will connect in some way to yours. Hopefully it will help each of us know what unique gifts we have to offer to this beautiful tapestry of life. I know that my story is enveloped in a larger one, the Story of the Universe. This knowledge—this gift—has made all the difference in my life.

I put pen to paper at the request of others. So often they have asked if I have ever thought of writing a book. I think they loved hearing the stories I told, stories about my life and experiences. They wanted to hold on to these stories, to remember and keep them.

Tell me a story. Children ask this from earliest childhood before they close their eyes in sleep. Sometimes they ask for the same story over and over again. The human heart loves to listen, and imagine different worlds with fascination. Somehow we feel most at home, most secure, most alive when enfolded and immersed in a story.

Although I know I can write fairly well, my real love is not writing, but *telling* the stories. Perhaps it is an Irish thing, passed on from my ancient Celtic heritage. There is something about being in a circle listening to the sound of a voice, looking into those expressive faces, and in the interaction see each story come alive, become real and live once again.

I also love to have a poem emerge. With sound and rhythm it captures the mysteries that live deep within us waiting for the space, the silence, the emotion to burst into being through language. Poems also have a voice. They are meant to be heard.

I hope that in reading this book, you can hear not only my voice, but the voice of the Universe calling to us to know that we are one, calling us to compassion and love, to celebration. There was a time in the evolutionary journey when there was no language, no voice to tell a story. I am grateful, looking into Deeptime, that language and story were born, that we can now remember, give thanks and celebrate. The human can communicate through centuries of discoveries. They can tell not only of discoveries but of deep feelings felt, and transformations of which they were a part. They can tell their stories. Even more amazing in recent history the human has discovered through science the story told by the Universe from its very beginning through the emergence of stars and galaxies and life on beautiful Earth, our home.

In the introduction to Brian Swimme and Thomas Berry's magnificent book *The Universe Story* are the words, "The goal is not to read a book; the goal is to read the story taking place all around us."[1] I read their book and listened deeply to their communication. It helped me to read the story taking place all around me. I hope in reading this book, you may discover how important you are, how unique. I hope too that you discover the story taking place all around you.

---

1. Brian Swimme and Thomas Berry, *The Universe Story: From the Primordial Flaring Forth to the Ecozoic Era—A Celebration of the Unfolding of the Cosmos* (New York: HarperCollins, 1992), 3.

I write this book for the children and the young of every species. I hope that in some small way these stories and actions that come from them may enable them to, as the beautiful songwriter Carolyn McDade puts it, *"Continue, continue, continue, continue. O let them continue on."*[2]

2. "Longing Suite" by Carolyn McDade, copyright ©2001 Carolyn McDade. All rights reserved. Used by permission.

· 1 ·

I'm Home

I'm on Long Island, looking out over the ten acres called Homecoming Farm. The world is in crisis: droughts, fires, hurricanes, floods, the Amazon burning. There are refugees all around us fleeing war, hunger, poverty. Some have lost their homes due to climate disruption, their homes washed into the sea. The coronavirus pandemic has caused all of us to stop, to listen, and wake from our illusions. The country is polarized, separation everywhere. Enemies to be hated and destroyed, competition rampant, consumerism still the national hallmark, racism and gender inequality still a part of the fabric of a country some call the greatest on Earth. We cannot seem to let go of the ranking of things, people, and countries. Separation leads us to such folly.

In the midst of all this chaos I am at peace. Gratitude fills my heart. It is a mystery I once tried to "figure out" by finding some rational explanation. How can I experience paradise with so much pain and suffering, so much hatred and cruelty, so much desperation in the world? My eyes take in a relatively small parcel of land once covered with grass, but now rows of lettuce, bok choy, radishes, turnips, seeds bursting into flowers and vegetables of so many different varieties. I have come home to this place where separation is no more, only communion.

It all began for me with a story, a New Story, not new at all really, just unobserved, hidden, and covered over with illusions we thought were real.[1] Those of us searching for the truth of things have come together. Scientists and people from the deep spiritual traditions of all religions are beginning to see together, to embrace spirit and mystery. Quantum physics and mysticism, once seen as separate, are now experienced by many of us as one. And this is not a lofty thing, not based in intellect and ideas, but based in the real, in soil and microbes, in earthworms, bees, and ants, in wind and birds and trees, in the water that gives life to all. It is based in the reality of energy becoming matter, of stars and sun, galaxies and Earth, all part of incarnation and communion.

I still experience fear and anger and the pain of grief and loss. The state of the world still causes me to weep. But the fabric of my life, its meaning and the story that holds it all together, has gifted me with a new identity. I am not separate or alone in life. I am connected to everything that is. I belong and am at home and that has made all the difference.

~

As I sit here looking out over the land, I am grateful for more than twenty-five years here at Homecoming Farm. They have been filled with connection and communion, but also struggles, with times when we thought we could never make it through. We have worked, celebrated, and learned together, all of us: the Dominican Sisters who gifted the land and gave their support; the families and friends who trusted in a new way of doing agriculture; the farmers who came, some just learning, and others who discovered farming was not for them; the interns who came to understand that farming is very hard work in heat and cold and on rainy harvest days. They learned, too, that crops sometimes fail, and that growth and life depend on sun and rain and the nurturance of soil.

---

1. Thomas Berry, "The New Story," *Teilhard Studies* 1 (Winter 1978). Online: https://thomasberry.org/the-new-story/.

As I look out over the fields, I think of Elizabeth Keihm, who joined me so many years ago and has shared the journey of Homecoming Farm with all its ups and downs. Her dedication, gifts, and talent, her love of life, soil, and beauty has blessed this land and made of it a sanctuary. She has given sanctuary to the bees and insects, reverence for the herbs and flowers, knowledge to the children and teens who have followed her around the farm and learned about each plant, unique and special, how each one grows and what it means to be organic. She also shared her knowledge of the life and habits of bees and ants, which helps us humans to know how much they help Earth and give to us an example of community.

The pages that follow are filled with stories that have led me home. But we are all in this together. My story and yours are all a part of the whole. The stories of our ancestors, both human and more than human, are part of us. They live on in a Universe filled with creativity and meaning. The unborn future ones are with us too, calling us to fidelity.

The memories contained in this book end here at Homecoming Farm. Looking back I can see that these stories sprinkled throughout my life have led me here to this place and all that has been created here. It is in a sense a final chapter.

My intuition tells me that this book should begin with this final chapter, the coming home to this place and—as T. S. Eliot said—We shall not cease from exploration / And the end of all our exploring / Will be to arrive where we started / And know the place for the first time.[2]

I have known this plot of land in Amityville on Long Island since I entered the congregation of the Sisters of St. Dominic

2. T. S. Eliot, *Complete Poems and Plays of T. S. Eliot* (New York: Faber, 1969), 197. From "Little Gidding," Part V.

in 1958. That's well over sixty years ago. But in 1992, when I returned here after studying at Genesis Farm, where I learned the teachings of Thomas Berry, I began to know this place for the first time. And I realize now that the journey through all these stories has led me here, back to the place where I started, the place that I thought I knew and to the person I thought I was, and now to know this place and myself for the first time.

As I look out over the ten acres of land, now saved in perpetuity, I am amazed at all that has led to this moment. I am grateful to Thomas Berry, who taught me that community is so much larger and so much more beautiful than I could have imagined. He taught that "There is no such thing as 'human community.'"[3] There is only the life community of which the human is a part.

The spiritual life is often spoken of as the journey home to the true self. I have—with the help of Thomas Berry, Miriam MacGillis (founder of Genesis Farm), and Brian Swimme—come to know a much larger self than the small one I thought I knew. This larger self is in reality the Universe, conscious of itself. This discovery will take the rest of my life to be with, and to understand at deeper and deeper levels. With the help of others who have come to this new understanding, I will learn to align my consciousness with the dynamic Universe and live my life in alignment with the life of Earth and Universe.

We are so gifted to be living at this moment in Earth's history; a moment that calls us to go deep and discover the gifts of creativity we have been given not for ourselves but for the continuation of life itself. For those who are looking for meaning and purpose larger than themselves, the mystics of all religious traditions and the scientists who are each day searching for truth give us the path in which to find this meaning. It is a jour-

---

3. Thomas Berry CP, with Thomas Clarke SJ, *Befriending the Earth: A Theology of Reconciliation between Humans and the Earth* (New London, CT: Twenty-Third Publications, 1991), 43.

ney worth taking, a journey into the truth. It will not always be easy or comfortable, but it will be rich and nourishing, exciting and adventurous, filled with the unknown and with unimaginable discoveries. It will be a journey filled with glimpses of paradise. It is a path of liberation asking us to go all the way in; all the way into the truth, into the knowledge that we are born from Earth, that all the elements in our bodies were first in a star and every creation from the smallest insect to the largest galaxy have the same origin story. It is everyone's story and this new discovery of ours has the possibility of forming us into a new kind of human, creating a world where the human lives in mutuality with all of life.

Resistance and Contemplation: Vermont

Vermont holds a very special place in my story. A contemplative order of Benedictine brothers and priests have their priory in Weston. In 1978, on one of my week-long stays, I went to morning prayer. It must have been in late autumn or winter, because the prayer was held not in the chapel but in a smaller room. I remember a potbelly stove with a fire going.

Morning prayer was one of my favorite times at the priory. Our prayer began before dawn in the darkness. The sun rose as the prayer continued, a very special time. When morning prayer finished and the brothers left, I stayed. I don't remember if the story of Moses and the burning bush was the reading of the day, but I began a meditation on it. I wondered what it really meant to come close to that fire. My meditation was filled with images of fire. I was drawn to stay in this place, feeling like I could not leave.

I went to the bookcase. One book jumped out at me as if it was put right in my hand. Its title spoke to me, *Resistance and Contemplation*. The author was James Douglass. When I opened it to the first chapter I read, "A way of liberation passes through fire."[1]

---

1. James W. Douglass, *Resistance and Contemplation: The Way of Liberation* (New York: Doubleday, 1972), 15.

I read the whole book sitting there in that place. It was not a big book, just a small paperback, but to read the whole thing—when I look at it now—was quite something, because it's not exactly light reading. What captured me in 1978 were the questions, Just how far would you like to go in?[2] How far into the truth? How far into liberation?

When I entered the Dominican Order in 1958, the motto of *Veritas* (truth) was a deep attraction. My other allurement was contemplation, as the Dominicans express it, "To contemplate and to give to others the fruit of your contemplation." Little did I know as a young woman that the journey to the truth and the gift of contemplation would lead to resistance and jail. That morning as I digested the words in Jim Douglass's book, I knew that the fire of truth was calling me to my own liberation. For so long I had wrestled with the reality of war, especially nuclear weapons. At this moment there was a Trident submarine being built in Groton, Connecticut. What I needed to do became clear to me on that morning in Vermont.

I came home and made an appointment with the sisters on the council of my congregation to talk about this call to resistance. I knew that I would have to have a concrete plan so that together we would be able to know the next steps. I had a friend in Nashville, Tennessee, Carol Feeney. She was a Dominican sister who was heading up their chapter of Clergy and Laity Concerned, an organization founded by Dr. Martin Luther King Jr. I had recently talked to Carol and knew that the sister with whom she was living had just moved, so she now had space in her apartment.

I presented my plan to the council. I would move to Nashville, live with Carol, and be connected to the work of Clergy and Laity Concerned, while at the same time immersing myself in the facts related to the Trident submarine. Carol and I would

---

2. Douglass, *Resistance and Contemplation*, 48.

be faithful to the Dominican way of life, engaging in study and seeking truth. We would live lives of contemplation while acting for justice and living together in community. I knew I would need to earn some money, so I proposed finding a part-time job.

It did not take long for the sisters on the council to decide. We spoke for about an hour, exchanged thoughts and ideas, and I knew in this brief amount of time that my congregation would send me forth to follow what I knew was a call as real as the one I had answered in 1958 when I entered the Dominican order. There was never a doubt in my mind that this path that had opened for me would lead me further into the truth. I would need to answer the question over and over again, how far in do you want to go?

· 3 ·

Nashville, and a Different Kind of Music

I knew Nashville was the home of country music, but during my years in Nashville I was never attracted to the Grand Ole Opry. My heart and soul were allured by a different kind of music. It was a music made together by a group of people trying to be faithful to the truth; joining our hands in a circle of commitment to justice, and loving the dance.

I loved living with Carol Feeney, with her passion and love of people and life. She was a born community organizer, and she gifted me with a ready-made community of people in Nashville. They became my source of hope and challenged me to stay faithful to the call to liberation and the fire of love, which also lived in the soil and the heart of Nashville. I was ignorant in the late seventies that John Lewis was one of the organizers of the sit-ins at the lunch counters in downtown Nashville in 1960, where he risked so much for truth. Of course I knew about the sit-ins, but was unaware that they took place in the very city where I now found myself searching for a way to tell the truth about the Trident submarine. The courage and commitment of people like John Lewis and those who joined with him in challenging the structural racism in our country had planted seeds of resistance and liberation that lived on in Nashville and somehow would, without my knowledge at the time, be a part of my own liberation.

The first thing I did when I arrived from New York, after unpacking my bags and taking up residence in the simple apartment that I would share with Carol, was look for a part-time job. What could I do that would bring in some income while providing space and time for the study I wanted to do? I came to the conclusion that my background in the education of children would give me the credentials and provide the references that would enable me to ask a couple to entrust me with the care of their child. I couldn't imagine that a parent would look for such a person through a newspaper advertisement, but I took the chance and took out a small ad in the Nashville newspaper. Within a day I received a call and set up an interview with a couple who lived in Belle Meade, an affluent suburb of Nashville.

That was the beginning of experiencing a hands-on lesson in what it means to live on the margins. It was the beginning of going into a truth that I had not seen or known before; beginning to know how resistance to the Trident submarine and the action and work of John Lewis were deeply connected at their roots.

I was hired by the couple to care for two beautiful little children, a boy about age five, and a little girl around three. Each morning I would board the bus in downtown Nashville and travel as the only white person into Belle Meade, a community of manicured lawns and flowers, of huge, beautiful houses. Their children, lawns, and upkeep were cared for by the people on the bus with me. There would be two or three buses each morning taking us into this suburb of Nashville and two or three buses taking us out before five or six p.m., when the buses ceased running. And I knew that I had a choice of remaining in Belle Meade, or else of traveling by car instead of bus, and being welcomed fully into one of those beautiful homes. Having the choice, however, I also knew that I would rather continue on the bus. Somehow— without my knowledge—the spirit of John Lewis was traveling with me and calling me deeper into the truth.

• 4 •

El Salvador Comes to Nashville

In trying to organize my thoughts for this book and putting my stories together, I came to a realization I had not known before. That realization was the discovery of how much the soil of Nashville enriched and influenced my actions.

I had a goal in mind when I journeyed to Tennessee to live with Carol Feeney. It was the next step, a place to be in order to reflect and study and actually find out where I was meant to go and what I was meant to do. I had no idea that the people of El Salvador would lead the way. That began to happen when the revelations about El Salvador came to Nashville.

Clergy and Laity Concerned was sponsoring a campaign the year I moved there to bring to Nashville people who were traveling to El Salvador, exploring the situation on the ground there and reporting back to the citizens in the United States. At that time the United States was heavily invested in El Salvador, supporting a government that was oppressing its own people. The truth about El Salvador exploded, and the eyes of the American people could no longer look away when Archbishop Óscar Romero was assassinated on March 24, 1980, while saying Mass in the small chapel of Divine Providence. It happened shortly after he had preached on that Sunday in the Cathedral of San Salvador, ordering the soldiers to put down their guns and stop killing their brothers and sisters. Nine months later four churchwomen, Sisters Ita Ford, Maura Clarke, Dorothy Kazel, and lay missionary Jean Donovan were raped, brutally murdered, and buried in a shallow grave in El Salvador.

Our little group organized through Clergy and Laity Concerned decided to go to Washington, DC, and the Pentagon to register our objection.

Nonviolent action has within it many surprises. Once in Washington, I blocked a ramp entrance from the basement mall-like floor of the Pentagon leading to the upper floors. I remember holding a sign, but I don't remember what it actually said. I wanted to communicate that I was there to interrupt business as usual.

Some time passed and I did not see them coming, but two men in three-piece suits came to us from an upper floor. As they passed me, each of them punched me pretty hard in my lower back. I remained standing there, holding my sign. A security guard observed me the whole time, and I knew he saw what had happened.

A few minutes later a man in a military uniform with quite a bit of brass on his shoulders approached and said to the guard, "Remove this woman; she is blocking the entrance."

To which the guard replied, "As long as you can get around her, you move, sir."

I could not believe my ears, nor the courage and integrity of this man. I knew he was risking more than me, more than jail. He was risking his livelihood. After this I was taken to jail for the first time, and I carried the image and the words of that courageous man with me.

El Salvador had come to Nashville and called me to the Pentagon. A security guard hired to keep order there saw a truth and responded. I heard again the words from *Resistance and Contemplation:* "Just how far would you like to go in?"[1]

The following is an article published in a newsletter of the Dominican Sisters. I was asked to write it explaining why I had gone to jail.

---

1. Douglass, *Resistance and Contemplation,* 46.

Speaking Hard Truth the Christian Way

The deputy called my name and said that I had visitors. Who could it be? I knew the last members of my community had gone back to Tennessee. As I walked into the visiting room I saw on the other side of the glass Ernie, Margaret, and Mary, my sisters from Hope House. The tears came for the first time since I had been arrested; tears not of sorrow but of deep joy. And I remembered hearing words spoken to me by Dan Berrigan. They were there living before me. *"Where faith is concerned, geography is very important. By that I mean where one stands."*

We stood there together in Richmond, Virginia, separated by glass. Margaret had brought five books with her, by Archbishop Hélder Câmara, Dietrich Bonhoeffer, Dorothy Day, Thomas Merton, and Dan Berrigan.

We stood together with these great ones and with those suffering in Central America; with Dorothy Day's poor remembering the Holocaust not over but in our midst. We stood with Merton coming out of a monastic tradition, contemplatives. We stood with Dan and the challenge of resistance. The books told the whole story of where I was standing and why. And my sisters stood with me. It was a moment of integrity and wholeness. It was a sacramental moment, and once again the word was made flesh.

I went to jail that the word might once again be made flesh. I put my body at the entrance to the Pentagon so that those going in to do the business of the day would be interrupted by my body. I went to jail because I am convinced that the arms race is against God's will, and in order to be divinely obedient I had to do civil disobedience.

Guilty of No Crime

Even as I reflect on the recent events of my life; my act of civil disobedience, my arrest and days in jail, I realize that our country is involved in another war; this time in El Salvador. The Department of "Defense" is supposedly defending our national security by sending military personnel, weapons, and money to aid a government that has no regard for human rights and that is responsible for the slaughter of thousands of its people.

I am reminded of the statement I made to the magistrate in the courtroom in Virginia shortly after my arrest. "I did what I am accused of doing. I blocked an entrance to the Pentagon. But I am guilty of no crime. The Pentagon commits crimes against humanity every day. We must see the crime of spending billions of dollars for weapons of death; dollars that could be used for food, shelter, and health care. We must see the crime committed by the Pentagon against people of other countries; the people of El Salvador."

In these times it is difficult to be an American. To be Christian involves saying and doing things that to some seem un-American. I believe that we are called to be faithful, and in our faithfulness to the truth transformation will come. We cannot allow ourselves to be co-opted by something some call American. We are called not to be American but to be faithful to the gospel.

I am deeply grateful to sisters for the telegrams and letters, for your support and understanding. I am deeply grateful too for those who do not understand, but who wrote to say, "We love you." Perhaps in time, because of our love, we will all be able to understand one another, and the geography that separates us will come together in a faith that allows us to stand together.

On the night before I was arrested, I slept at the foot of the altar in the sanctuary of St. Stephen Martyr Church in Washington, DC. I woke early in the morning; it was still dark. I was filled with a deep peace; and as I looked at the sanctuary lamp burning and the stained-glass windows, I knew from whence I had come. I knew that I would go to do what I had to do; I would break the law. I knew that I would do this act not in my own name, nor out of any leftist political ideals. As I woke in the silence of that morning, the last day of 1980, I knew that I was coming from the church.

• 5 •

Love Pierces through the Walls

Tennessee State Prison, a maximum-security facility in Nashville, is often referred to as The Walls. It is a place to lock up, lock down, lock in people that society deems dangerous, and to lock out anything beautiful. Somehow in the course of things, truth and compassion find their way into such places in unexpected ways, and the walls give way to love.

During the few short years I spent in Nashville, I spent some time each week behind the Walls, going with a beautiful elderly woman named Everlina to pray with the men whose lives had led to lockup in this place surrounded by walls. Each week I got to know these men whom I never in the course of my life would have ever met, and by no means would have ever entered into glimpses of their relationship with God. I know that some of the men who came to pray each Tuesday night came just to get out of their cell for a while, maybe find some release from boredom or isolation. But each Tuesday night something happened as we all met, asked how we were doing, and related to one another as something more than a number. No matter what reason drew each one of these men to come each week, a space opened up, a crack in the walls, love entered in. I have been a part of many groups who prayed together, but I had never witnessed prayer the way I had behind these walls. I was changed.

One day here in this state penitentiary I attended Mass with the incarcerated men. It was on this day that I would be brought to tears and would learn a song that would remain with me and connect me to these men in ways I never would have dreamed. During Mass about six men, all Black, stood with their backs to the people gathered there. They stood to sing a song. All I saw were the numbers on their backs as I listened to a song I had never heard before:

> I ain't in no way tired.
>> Come so far from where I started from.
> Nobody told me the road would be easy.
>> I don't believe God brought me this far to leave me.
> No I don't believe God brought me this far to leave me.[1]

I knew I had to learn the song, and so when Mass was ended I approached the piano player and asked him to teach it to me. I don't remember if it was he who told me, or if I had learned it later from another source, but someone told me that it was a song coming out of the experience of slavery. I know the song spoke to me on a very deep level.

---

1. James Cleveland recorded the best-known version of this song in 1978, with the lyrics "I Don't Feel No Ways Tired." Sister Jeanne Clark remembers it being sung the way she has written it (Curtis Burrell, "I Don't Feel No Ways Tired," Savgos Music, Inc., Peermusic III Ltd.).

Betrayal (Summer 1979)

Mourning, grieving, dying me
   aware
Illusions gone
Memory splintered into pieces of painful
   looks at lies
Fragments of a dream believed once.

I mourn the loss of innocence
I grieve and bear the guilt of taking part
   in the illusion
"Tell your people"
"Tell your people"
Cries from El Salvador, the Philippines
   the poor
They speak the truth that makes us free
But first the grief; the lonely, anguished season
   of betrayal.

Disturbing the Peace

I used to say yes when I meant no just to keep the peace.
Disturbing things is such a messy business.
You lose some friends and those who once thought of you
as polite and quite acceptable
Now view you as a troublemaker.

Disturbing things is unacceptable as occupation.
We cling to order and security even if that order
Crushes in its top-heaviness.
And our spirits sink so low we try to bring them
Back to life by buying things.
We try to keep the peace and say that everything's
All right even if our children are committing suicide.

I'm happy to be disturber of the peace
Although at times it's lonely and I yearn to feel
more a part of things.
It's frightening to disturb myself and stir within me
Things that were quite content to live with someone else's
*   answers*
Rather than my own integrity.

At times I shield myself and close my eyes and ears to those
Who would disturb my peace.
Forgive me.
Instead I should give thanks for cries for help,
For photos of charred flesh of children burned by US foreign
*   policy.*

Ugliness revealed disturbs my peace
Thank God.
If only all of us were disturbers of the peace
There'd be some hope for children and for fragile things
crushed within the present order.
If we disturbed our peace Earth would sing
And air would become fresh again.

Maybe in disturbing one another we'd find a way
To live together without grasping and without weapons
And our peace would be deserving of being undisturbed.

• 6 •

Good Friday

Usually the liturgy for Good Friday is not conducted at the Pentagon. But on Good Friday in 1981, I found myself there with a community of people who believed that connecting the Pentagon and crucifixion was a way of telling the truth.

Archbishop Romero had been assassinated in March of 1980, and the four churchwomen in December of that year. Thousands of Salvadoran people, including many children, were killed by a government the United States was supporting in El Salvador. At noon on Good Friday 1981, I poured blood on the post that held the plaque that said "Department of Defense" while the community chanted "This is the blood of the poor, this is the blood of El Salvador, this is the blood of Christ." I was handcuffed and led away by a security guard and placed in a bus along with another woman from the community who had done the same on another post at the river entrance of the Pentagon.

I remember it was quite a large bus just for the two of us; perhaps they were expecting more people to be arrested. But while we waited for that bus to leave for the courthouse, with the two security guards who had put us in handcuffs, the song I had learned at the state penitentiary in Nashville came back to me and I began to sing:

> I ain't in no way tired
>   Come so far from where I started from.

Nobody told me the road would be easy.

I don't believe God brought me this far to leave me.

No I don't believe God brought me this far to leave me.

The two security guards looked at me knowingly, and I knew they recognized the song. We were on that bus together, not as prisoner and guard, but as people who needed liberation.

The guards had come from a people enslaved, and now all of us, all the people were enslaved by weapons and war, by power and greed, by separation and cruelty. I was getting close to the truth, close to the fire, close to the burning bush and liberation. How far in did I want to go?

Our next stop was court. I testified that day, Good Friday, and from the witness stand told the court why I had come to the Pentagon. I began by saying that in our churches the people were singing on this day "Were you there when they crucified my Lord?" and recounted the many ways the Pentagon was involved in the crucifixion.

I was found guilty.

I can't remember exactly what my charge was. I'm sure it was related to destruction of property, because the prosecutor asked the judge to charge me with a felony and a year in prison, since as he put it, "The red substance they pour on the pillar needs to be sandblasted off, and it is destructive to the building." The judge refused his request and sentenced me to thirty days in the DC jail.

While waiting in a room right off the courtroom, the security guard who had brought me to court came in to thank me for what I had done. I was reminded of the other security guard who had watched me be punched while nonviolently protesting, and later stood with me. We were standing together, those inside and outside the Pentagon. The truth asks us to stand somewhere, and we were choosing to stand together.

I was put in leg irons, chained at the waist, and then hand-cuffed to that waist chain. I asked the man who was putting me in chains if he thought I was so dangerous that I had to be put in leg irons.

"Oh no," he said, "I heard you testify in the courtroom."

"Then why?" I asked.

He replied, "It's my job. I'm just doing my job."

I know that the man putting me in chains did not think I was dangerous. But there were those who knew the danger of my action and my words. Truth telling is dangerous to a system where truth is the enemy.

Sister Jeanne being arrested at the Pentagon.
(Photographer unknown)

• 7 •

The White Train

Sister Carol Feeney and I decided to travel from Nashville to Berea, Kentucky, to attend a program in which Father Daniel Berrigan would be reading his poetry. Little did I know at the time that the decision to attend this program would be a life-changer for me.

I really don't remember much about hearing Dan's poetry. What I will never forget is a story told by a woman, Mary, who at the time looked to be about seven months pregnant. It was the story of Franz Jägerstätter, an Austrian peasant living at the time of Hitler. Against the advice of his priest and bishop, he refused to fight in Hitler's army. Because of that decision he was put into prison and eventually beheaded. During his time in prison, the chaplain asked him why he had made this decision. Jägerstätter told the chaplain about a dream he had. It was a dream about a shining, white train. Everyone in the country was boarding the train, and he too boarded. As he was sitting on the train, he heard screams and asked the person next to him about the screams.

"Don't you know where this train is going?" the person answered. "This train is going to hell."

Franz Jägerstätter knew he had to get off the train. The train represented National Socialism in Germany at the time, and he had to get off.

I knew I was on a train, not in Nazi Germany, but here in the United States of America.

23

I remember it was dark when Carol and I drove back to Nashville. During the ride I talked to her about Franz Jägerstätter's dream and the White Train. I told her about my feeling that we were all on that train, and it was not National Socialism in Germany but participating in the nuclear arms race. I knew I had to get off. But why would I get off if everyone was on the train? I knew if I got off, I would have to get in front of it, to stop it. It was a powerful image for me, and I lived with it for many years not realizing that the image was leading me, guiding me to Ground Zero for Nonviolent Action and the home of the Trident submarine.

In Memory of and Gratitude to Franz Jägerstätter, Óscar Romero, Jean Donovan, Ita Ford, Maura Clark, and Dorothy Kazel

*You gave your life in love
Sacrifice embedded into wholeness
Became food for me
Energy for action*

*You gave your life
And sight was given me
An opening to find my way back home*

*I celebrate your life and your self-giving
A reason for rejoicing and for hope*

*The story carries on
Expanding to include all the acts of courage
and of bravery
Acts of solidarity*

*The sun who gives its life and energy away
To nourish soil and seed and all of life
On this beloved planet
Burns on
And so do I*

• 8 •

Jail Opened Up the Journey

My sojourn in the DC jail was a time for remembering from whence I had come, while considering where I would go. My monastic roots were revealed and became solace during a time of isolation. I remembered that my room in the convent was called a cell. It was a small place with a bed, a small desk, a sink, and a closet that held one clean habit. I had two habits (the term we used for the long garb we wore), one to wear and one to wash, ready for a change. There was never any decision, so clothing was no preoccupation.

So, too, in the DC jail. An orange jumpsuit was all there was, with no decision to be made. My cell had no desk, but it did provide a place for me to be alone with plenty of time for reflection. And because I was familiar with the word *horarium*, or order of the day, I made a schedule for myself: a time for reading, then meditation, exercise, and writing, ways to pass the nights and days.

However, there was a difference from the quiet of the convent. Jail had constant noise and loud music that I tried to filter out, with great difficulty. I fasted for my 30 days in jail (actually 28 since I got two days off for "good behavior," whatever that might mean). I did take juice once a day, since I wanted to be sure my body would survive the time with little physical disability since it was a bit unknown what might happen if I felt faint or worse.

Each morning I traveled to the infirmary with women who were on methadone. They took it with orange juice. I went to meals even though I was fasting, just to be with others. It gave me time to exchange some words and explain what I was doing in this place. I also gave my meal away, which helped me gain some favor with those few women with whom I interacted.

Once a day or so our cell doors were opened for a time of "recreation." After a few days of getting to know who was who, some women asked if I would pray with them. That was a very special time, a chance for me to hear the stories from these women's lives, many about their children. I learned that most of them were there because of prostitution, or because they signed bad checks.

This brought back memories I had of spending time in a courtroom in Brooklyn, when I was campus minister at Long Island University. I had accompanied a student in trouble. We sat for hour upon hour in the courtroom, waiting for something to happen. I noticed so many women charged with prostitution. Where were the men who had used them? Those men did not seem to appear in court. Now here I was, years later, surrounded by similar women whose names I now knew, and who were telling me about their children. I prayed with them and for their children. I felt free in jail because I chose to go there. These women were not so privileged, and freedom was far from what they felt or would ever experience. I was humbled by their presence in the time I spent with them.

On one of my visits in the DC jail I learned that Jim Douglass was also in jail on the West Coast, for a six-month sentence. I reflected on how this person, Jim, whom I had not yet met, was the reason I too was here in jail. He had left me with that question still ringing in my ears, "How far in do you want to go?" I wrote to Jim and told him where I was and why.

Sometime later when I was back in New York, I noticed a pamphlet saying Jim would speak in Pittsburgh. I knew I had to get there. I traveled by car the long distance to Pittsburgh with my friend Margaret. There I met Jim, and he told me my letter was in his briefcase. He was sorry he had not yet responded. Then he pulled out a draft of a pamphlet he was preparing for distribution at Ground Zero, a place he and Shelley, his wife, had founded. On the pamphlet was a picture of a boxcar of a train with words underneath the picture "Trident is the Auschwitz of Puget Sound." These words were from Raymond Hunthausen, then archbishop of Seattle. I recalled hearing the story of Franz Jägerstätter and the White Train, back when I attended that conference in Berea, Kentucky.

I knew I was on that train, and for me it was being part of the nuclear arms race. There was no doubt in my mind that I would travel to Ground Zero. The image of the train and the words of Archbishop Hunthausen were leading me there.

What Is Trident?
A Meditation by Jim Douglass

Trident is the end of the world.

Trident is a nuclear submarine which with Trident 2 missiles is able to destroy 192 cities or areas at one time, each with a blast 38 times more powerful than the Hiroshima bomb. Trident is 7,296 Hiroshimas. One Trident submarine can destroy any country on Earth. The fleet of Trident submarines (18 in the United States, 4 in the United Kingdom) can end life on Earth.

I don't understand.

> Good. We're getting somewhere. What is it you don't understand?

A submarine which equals 7,296 Hiroshimas. How can anyone understand that?

Begin with a meditation. To understand Trident say the word "Hiroshima." Reflect on its meaning for one second. Say and understand "Hiroshima" again. And again. And again. 7,296 times. Assuming you're able to understand Hiroshima in one second, you'll need more than two hours to understand Trident. That's one Trident submarine. To understand the destructive power of the entire Trident fleet, it would take you more than sixteen hours, devoting one second to each Hiroshima.

From James Douglass, *Lightning East to West* (New York: Crossroad, 1983). Used with permission of the author.

Your meditation is impossible. To understand Hiroshima alone would take a lifetime.

> You *do* understand. Hiroshima was the end of our ability to imagine our destructive power, or to measure its consequences. Trident is the end of the world.

How does one live at the end of the world?

> By beginning a new one. Stop Trident and open up a new world.

You've lost me again. Stopping Trident does sound like beginning a new world—not a very feasible goal. I think you need therapy. You need to adjust to a world that is a long way from stopping Trident.

> What we all need is not therapy but the vision of Gandhi, and Jesus before him, who show the way to turn an end of the world into the beginning of a new one.

You mean the power of nonviolent resistance and loving one's enemies?

> Yes.

What about the power of Trident?

> The power of Trident comes from the grip of an illusion, our own egos and the murderous security they seek. The force of truth and love lived in their depths is a force of unity, of life itself. That force is real. We need to test the truth of love by betting our lives on it in the world. If a community can experiment deeply enough in a nonviolent love-force, Trident will be stopped. Love will stop Trident.

• 9 •

Ground Zero

"And we'll all breathe together . . ."[1]

In late November of 1981 I traveled by car across the county to the state of Washington to join a group of people at Ground Zero Center for Nonviolent Action. They were organizing to resist the arrival of the first Trident submarine, the USS *Ohio.*

A few years later, I and three others who were helping to organize a protest upon the arrival of a train carrying weapons to the Trident were charged with conspiracy.

Conspiracy is usually thought of as doing something with others secretively—something against the law. At Ground Zero we never kept secrets, and we challenged any law that would allow a weapon like Trident to exist. At the same time that we were charged, the government was also charging people at a Baptist church in Seattle with conspiracy for harboring Salvadoran refugees inside the church. Together we planned a large gathering in that church. It would take place after the trial of nineteen people who knelt in front of a train carrying nuclear weapons to the Trident submarine base at Bangor, Washington, on the Kitsap Peninsula.

It was a beautiful gathering of hundreds of people. A Chilean band played as people entered the church, enlivening everyone. A creative musician named Steve Kinzie wrote a song for the occasion, reminding all of us of the meaning of the word

---

1. Steve Kinzie, "Breathe Together" (song), used by permission.

31

"conspire"—con-spire—to breathe together. Some of the lines of the song were "And we'll all breathe together, to break these chains of death, conspiring in the spirit until we all run out of breath." Steve's wife, Debbie Roberts, who speaks Spanish, participated in the journey of accompaniment that brought the Salvadoran family of thirteen to that sanctuary. Suzanne Smith, one of the jurors who had found the defendants not guilty, was there to celebrate and breathe together with us.

ᔐ

This past Holy Week in 2021 as I watched the trial of Derek Chauvin, the police officer accused of murdering George Floyd, I thought of the last words George Floyd spoke, "I can't breathe."[2] Breath is such a precious thing, and to be deprived of it by others speaks of an alienation from life and all its meaning. I felt watching this trial that many of us around the country and world were breathing together to change the systems that bind us all in an inhumanity of division, hatred, and racism. I hope beyond all hope that we are given time to change, to be involved in this conspiracy of love and breathing together so that none of us can say "I can't breathe" because of the action of another or a system that takes our breath away, choking us to death.

Many of us who meditate follow our breath in and out in order to be present to the present moment. We are actually breathing in the same air that travels the Earth, breathed by billions of people and animals living now or having lived in the past. Scientists estimate that some of the air we breathe takes two years to travel the whole Earth. We can imagine as we take our next breath that the air we are breathing in was breathed by other humans and animals living on Earth. It is in a sense one breath we are breathing. When George Floyd ran out of breath, so too did we.

---

2. Kevin Young, "Remembering George Floyd and the Movement He Sparked, One Year Later," National Museum of African-American History and Culture, May 25, 2021.

Arrival at Ground Zero

I arrived at Ground Zero in early December amid a rain that seemed never to stop. It took some getting used to, but the community of people with whom I would spend the next four-and-a-half years would compensate for any dreariness the rain would bring. I had picked up Rene in Cleveland and traveled with her the distance to Ground Zero. Karol and Marya had just arrived a short time before. We would be joined by two young couples and their children, George and Linda and little Christie, and Jim and Maggie and their infant son, Daniel.

Later we would add for a period of time a couple from Germany, Herbert and Anna. And of course all of us were there because of Jim and Shelley Douglass, who lived beside the railroad tracks leading into the Trident base.

My memories are many of those years at Ground Zero, with all the beautiful moments of life lived saying no to Trident and yes to life. We attempted to live out the philosophy of Gandhi and his concept of *satyagraha*, "truth-force" or "love-force." At the heart of all my memories is the theme of home. During my days, months, and years at Ground Zero, the theme of home emerged and has never left me to this day. Many of us wrote for the newspaper that we published. I often wrote about home, "On the Way Home," "Going Home," "Far from Home." I think the theme first came to me because the Bangor submarine base was called the "Homeport" of the Trident submarine. I knew the Trident could not possibly have a true home here on Earth.

But where was home? And how do we get there? Our actions as a community at Ground Zero were leading us to that place.

The Arrival of the USS *Ohio*

On August 12, 1982, the USS *Ohio*, America's first Trident submarine, traveled to the state of Washington to be fitted with weapons at the Bangor submarine base on the Kitsap Peninsula.

We had spent many months preparing and planning for its arrival. We had done retreats on the Olympic Peninsula, gathering people who would be willing to go into the waters of the Hood Canal. Later, because of actions of the Navy, the participants entered even more dangerous waters of the Strait of Juan de Fuca in the Pacific Ocean. I believe the final count of those who participated was 42 people. We would be in rowboats tied together as a human blockade, brought out by two large ships. The *Pacific Peacemaker* was a large sailboat that had traveled to the Kitsap Peninsula from Australia. There was also a catamaran called the *Lizard of Woz*.

On August 12 we got the message that the Trident was arriving. Another woman and I were on the *Pacific Peacemaker*, ready in our wetsuits to climb down into one of the rowboats. I asked Bill, the captain, to turn the boat so that we could see what was happening. As he did I saw a great deal of black smoke and lots of lights. Later we were told that the Coast Guard used 99 ships that day. As I looked out at the sight I thought, "They have declared war and we are the enemy; people (many of whom were women) with no shoes in rowboats." And I thought of all the wars conducted by the United States that had used tremendous firepower on people with no shoes.

The Coast Guard used high-powered water hoses to knock many of us into the water.[3]

Since we had presumed the Coast Guard would not rescue us from the waters of the Pacific Ocean, many people in boats witnessing what was happening, but not part of the blockade, came to our rescue and picked us up.

Seventeen people were arrested before they even got into their rowboats. They included Jim Douglass and those on the *Lizard of Woz* catamaran. Jim told us later that they boarded, and one

---

3. Martin Heerwald, "Trident Sub Reaches Home Port, Protesters Washed Away," *UPI Archives*, August 12, 1982.

young member of the Coast Guard held a gun, his hand shaking. In order to relieve the tension, Jim knelt and began the Our Father.

It took some time before I could speak. It took even longer to recover from the experience. I wanted to get to Seattle and be there with those who had been arrested. While waiting for the ferry to take me to Seattle, a reporter asked what I thought about all that had happened that day out in the Pacific Ocean. I shared with him the one thought that kept coming to me about the 99 Coast Guard ships, the smoke, the lights, and my understanding that it was a war . . . and we were the enemy. The reporter responded, "Yes, today they made war on the peacemakers." The charges against the seventeen people were dropped. I'm sure the government wanted no more truth to be told in the courtroom.

Connecting with
Franz Jägerstätter

It was December 8, 1982, and I was home alone. The phone rang. It was Jim Douglass calling from his home alongside the railroad tracks leading into the submarine base at Bangor. I listened as he recounted the content of a call he had just received from a reporter who had asked him the question, "Have you ever seen a white train? I just saw it traveling through a suburb outside of Seattle. I took a photo." Jim explained that he had never seen it, but knew from documents he had seen that if ever nuclear weapons were transported, they would be on a white train. As he was talking to the reporter, the train pulled slowly into the base as Jim watched out his window.

I was spellbound by this news and could not quite believe what I was hearing. It was Franz Jägerstätter's dream about the White Train that had brought me to Ground Zero, and now I was hearing the news that there actually *was* a white train that was carrying nuclear weapons to the Trident here on the Kitsap Peninsula. I remembered that I had said to my friend Sister Carol Feeney as we traveled back from Berea, Kentucky, to Nashville, Tennessee, that I knew I was on the train, and the train represented the nuclear arms race. I knew like Franz Jägerstätter that I had to get off the train.

"But why, if everyone was on the train," I said, "would I get off? I would only get off so that I could get in front of it. To stop it."

The train left the base after a few days, and we traced it back to Amarillo, Texas, where all nuclear weapons were assembled. We knew the train would travel back to the base at a future date.

There was no doubt in my mind where I would be when it arrived. I knew I would be in front of it.

• 11 •

His Name Is Daniel, and He's Asking Us to Stop the Train

It was on March 22, 1983, when the White Train carrying nuclear weapons traveled from the Pantex Plant in Amarillo, Texas, and returned again to the Bangor base. This time it would not come in silence.

The last time it came, only Jim Douglass witnessed it. Now there would be hundreds of people, and national press from as far away as New York. Six of us would be willing to risk arrest in order to go onto the tracks to be in front of the train, asking it to stop.

I decided to carry three things with me as I walked across the tracks to the final row on which the train would come. I carried my Bible, a bouquet of daffodils, and a picture of little Daniel— the son of Maggie and Jim, with whom I lived—who was then four months old.

As I started across the tracks, a young Kitsap County sheriff took my arm and told me to stop. I continued walking. He asked again, this time telling me that if I did not stop I would be arrested.

As I continued to walk I said to the officer, "I have to stop that train. The cargo on that train is going to kill us all."

The officer pushed me to the ground, where I remained kneeling.

We watched together as the White Train approached. I remember it was very silent as the crowd took in the look of the train, with its turrets, behind which were people ready to shoot if the train was threatened. Some who had made it to the last track were being arrested. The officer and I remained there together, he standing, me kneeling, seeing together for the first time this monstrosity. I remembered a line attributed to Dorothy Day about nuclear weapons: "Is there a difference between throwing innocent people into ovens and throwing ovens at innocent people?"[1] It was an extension of Franz Jägerstätter's train. For me the connection was clear, and I knew that Franz Jägerstätter's spirit had led me to these tracks and to this moment.

After the train passed, the officer told me I was under arrest. When he pushed me to the ground, the photo of Daniel fell out of my Bible.

I thought that maybe the officer was a young father, so I asked him if he saw the photo of the baby.

He sadly nodded his head, *Yes*.

I told him, "His name is Daniel, and he is asking us to stop the train."

I had to walk quite a distance from where I was to the sheriff's car waiting to take me off to jail. There were people all along the way as I walked, and I just kept showing the photo of Daniel and repeating over and over again, "His name is Daniel, and he's asking us to stop the train." Upon my arrival at the car, there stood Sheriff Jones, the person in charge of the officers. I showed the photo to him and repeated my message. He looked at me in such a knowing way. I knew he got the message, and understood.

As I tell this story, I realize that I am not sure that I was handcuffed. I don't remember. But I do remember holding that photo up one last time as I got into the police car, and saying for the final time, "His name is Daniel, and he's asking us to stop the train."

---

1. Although this quote has been repeatedly attributed to Dorothy Day in multiple books and by people who knew her, such as Art Laffin of the Dorothy Day Catholic Worker in Washington, DC, so far we have been unable to find the original source for it.

Sister Jeanne Clark holds the photo she carried when she was charged with "obstructing a lawfully operated train," though she knew, under international law, that the train operated illegally. Photo by Elizabeth Keihm, Executive Director of Homecoming Farm.

I was told later that KING–TV in Seattle aired that exact scene over and over again. Years later I learned that Glen Milner had been touched by seeing me on the TV news. He responded by being in front of the train two years later. He wrote these words on a vest that he wore as he knelt on the tracks: "I am here for the love of these children," referring to his two children, Alisa and Aaron (photo follows the next chapter).

The White Train had come to the Bangor base. But this time the people were there to see it, and to say *No.* I suspected that day that some among the sheriffs who arrested us also wanted to say, *No.* I knew it was a matter of time. The truth when spoken, like water through the cracks, finds ways to travel on.

I was in jail the day that Daniel was baptized. I wrote him this letter, which was read at the ceremony.

↪

Daniel, dearest child,

You truly have been a gift of God to me. I am very present to you today as you are welcomed into the Christian community. You call us to faithfulness.

We share with you today and for the days ahead our faith and hope. Faith in Jesus who taught us to serve one another; to care for one another; to be as little children and enter into the kingdom even now in the midst of a world that refuses to believe in life and in one another.

We pledge to you today our commitment to life, to you and all the children of the Earth. We say to you today that we have hope, a gift given to us by God through one another. We say to you today that we are a people who rejoice because of God's presence among us; a people willing to suffer because of our belief; people who trust in God's faithfulness to us.

Today we place you in the center of our community, Daniel, as you call us forth to be the Church.

I love you very much.
Auntie Jeanne

Poem

by Father Daniel Berrigan SJ

wondrously
the unknown
coincides
with the known
when on the way
knowing
is renounced.
The nun knelt down
before the ghost train
snaking its cargo
breathlessly, noiselessly
like a hellish midair
mutant
through the night.
Would death stop short
halt in its tracks?
No way of knowing.
Unknowing
undesirous of knowing

she knows only
(a preview
of beatific dawn)
who
goes
there

Daniel

Previously unpublished poem sent to Sister Jeanne by Dan Berrigan after her action in front of the White Train.

· 12 ·

The Kitsap County Courtroom, Another Place to Tell the Truth

"Do you swear to tell the truth, the whole truth, and nothing but the truth so help you God?"

"I do."

All of us know these words even if we have never been in a courtroom. We've heard them in films or on TV. Now I was on trial in Kitsap County in the state of Washington. The question was, did the court really want the truth, the whole truth, and nothing but the truth? My charge was "Obstructing a lawfully operated train." My defense? The train was not lawful since its cargo was nuclear weapons, which would be placed on the Trident submarine in violation of international law.

For all of us at Ground Zero, the truth was very clear. We wanted to bring that clarity to the jury. Often our judicial system tries to keep the truth out by declaring certain things irrelevant. In this trial the judge declared the cargo of the train and international law irrelevant, and therefore the jury would not be permitted to hear this defense.

When the judge takes away your defense, why even go to trial? This was the question we dealt with as a group as we awaited trial. How could we participate and remain silent in such a kangaroo court? We considered our options. Jim Douglass asked me if I had ever met Robert Aldridge, one of the lead designers of the Trident submarine. Aldridge resigned from Lockheed when he discovered that Trident was a first-strike weapon. I responded that I had met him and heard him speak about the Trident one evening at Ground Zero.

"How about Richard Falk?" Jim asked. I had never met him. He was Professor of International Law at Princeton University, I knew, and I had read an article he wrote in the *Seattle Post-Intelligencer*. He stated that when your country is involved in a crime, it is not only your right but your duty to protest. After considering my knowledge and the influence these two men had on my understanding of the Trident and my action, we decided that I could use the defense of "state of mind," which the judge could not take away from me. This would allow Robert Aldridge and Richard Falk to testify on my behalf and the jury would hear what I heard from these two men. Then the jury could know the truth.

Since I was representing myself, I called Robert Aldridge to the stand, knowing that the prosecuting attorney would object since the judge had taken both Aldridge and Falk off the witness list in his attempt to make them irrelevant. The prosecutor objected, and I responded by stating that Mr. Aldridge would testify as to my state of mind.

The judge then allowed him to take the stand. You can imagine the jury's curiosity as they learned who Robert Aldridge was. I asked him to tell the jury where he had worked, and what he had done at Lockheed. I then asked him to give the jury a synopsis of the talk he had given the night I was present at Ground Zero. He proceeded with no objection, and told the jury all about the Trident submarine and its first-strike capability. It was an historic moment.

I then called Richard Falk to the stand, and had the article he had written in the *Post-Intelligencer* entered into evidence. He then proceeded to tell the jury the contents of the article. I will never forget how he said, "We should not be asking, 'Did these people do the wrong thing?' We should be asking why we are not all doing the same." The truth had entered the courtroom. Now the question was how the jury and the judge would respond to that truth.

As the court proceedings continued, I took the stand. I tried to show the jury how knowing what I knew about the Trident submarine, as Robert Aldridge had just demonstrated for them, and the ethical and legal ramifications contained in Richard Falk's article, I had to be in front of that train to save the future for the children and the flowers. I carried the bouquet of daffodils and the photo of Daniel at four months old to be clear about why I was attempting to stop the train.

The prosecuting attorney then called the officer who had arrested me to the stand. He was a witness for the prosecution, but in many ways he was also my witness. The way he spoke about me, and the way he had written up his report of the arrest, was a testimony to the truth.

"She kept saying, 'I have to stop that train, that train is going to kill us all.' Her Bible fell to the ground. She knelt there. It appeared as though she was praying."

When I got a chance to cross examine the officer, I asked him if he remembered the photo of the baby. Then I showed it to him.

"Well I can't say that is the exact photo," he said. "But I think I just saw him outside in the hall."

Daniel's mom and dad had brought him to court, and he was right outside the door. The people in the courtroom laughed. Humanity entered in.

After a few hours of deliberation, the jury was hung. The judge asked if there was anything that would enable them to try to come to a consensus. They had two questions that they said would help if answered.

We went back into the courtroom as the judge read the two questions aloud: "Can we consider the cargo on the train?" and "Can we consider international law?" The jury had gotten to the core of our defense. However, the judge answered that they could not consider either the cargo or international law. The jury went back to deliberate, and in a short time came back with their verdict.

Guilty.

I don't remember if it was the next day or a few days after the trial ended, but I received a call from one of the jurors asking if he could come and talk to me. We set up a time and he came to my home.

"We didn't want to find you guilty" he said.

"Then why did you?"

"The judge gave us no choice."

I shared my belief that we always have a choice, and told him about what is called "jury nullification." He—like most people—knew nothing about it. So I gave him literature about it. Jury nullification happens when a jury chooses to ignore the law, because it believes that in this specific case the law is unjust.

The next time the White Train came to the submarine base, that member of the jury was standing there with us.

Trespass (May 3, 1988)

They call it trespass when we try to stop the crime
When we stand or kneel in front of trains
or doors of embassies and consulates
Places that support the war in language that is
meant to cover up

They say that we disturb the peace
We peacemakers who stand in front of doors
Saying that this business has to stop
Our conduct is disorderly when the order is death dealing

They know the truth and speak it sometimes
We do disturb their peace thank God
Willing too to disturb our own.

· 13 ·

Wouldn't You Go to Jail If It Would Help End the War?

More and more people were beginning to know about and to protest the White Train as it traveled across the country from Amarillo, Texas, to the Naval Submarine Base Bangor on the Kitsap Peninsula.

In June of 1985, nineteen people were on trial for kneeling on the tracks as the White Train approached the Trident submarine base. They were charged with trespassing.

I had been charged with conspiracy in this same action just for helping to organize this protest. Those charges were dropped, so I was able to go to the trial to observe the proceedings. It was a privilege to hear the powerful testimony of people committed to saying no to the Trident submarine and to the train that carried weapons that could end life on Earth.

Two of those testimonies will forever be in my memory. The first was the witness of Karol Schulkin, from our Ground Zero community. When asked why she decided to kneel in front of the train, she replied that when she was just eleven or twelve years old, the boy next door received a BB gun. She was excited to go outside with him to see how it worked. He gave her the gun so she could learn how to aim. She was practicing aiming the gun into a tree, when suddenly a little bird fell from it. She sadly learned at a very young age what it meant to target something.

The other reason she said she decided to be in front of the train was because of a plaque that for many years hung in her room. She actually brought it with her to enter into evidence. On

48

it were written these words: "Wouldn't you go to jail if it would help end the war?"

During the trial I sat next to Daniel Ellsberg. He came to testify as an expert, based on his previous work in analyzing and helping to devise nuclear war plans, but the judge removed him from the witness list, not allowing him a voice. During Karol's testimony I noticed that he began to weep.

Later, during a recess in the trial, a reporter approached him, "I noticed you became very emotional during Miss Schulkin's testimony. May I ask why?"

Daniel Ellsberg explained that he had participated in many trials, but he had never heard a witness quote his words from the stand. At the time that he had said those words, "Wouldn't you go to jail if it would help end the war?" he was facing many years in prison for releasing the Pentagon Papers to the press. As he was surrendering for arraignment, he had spoken those words in reply to a reporter who asked him whether he was worried about going to jail. He had wondered then if his actions would make any difference. He was very touched to hear someone—so many years later—quote his words as her reason for being in front of a train carrying nuclear weapons to the Trident submarine.

The last person to testify in the trial was Glen Milner, an electrician, who lived in Seattle. Glen responded to the question of why he had knelt in front of the train by explaining that he and his wife Karol had been deciding whether to have a third child. At first he thought he didn't want to bring another child into the world with so much violence, war, and nuclear weapons. But he realized how hopeless that position was, so he said, "I was in front of the train to earn the right to give birth to this child."

His defense lawyer asked, "But why this action? Why the train?"

Sitting next to Daniel Ellsberg, I found it was now my turn to cry as Glen explained, "Two years ago I was watching TV in my home in Seattle. The first White Train had just arrived at the base. I saw a woman being arrested and put into the police car.

Glen Milner and his children.

She was holding up a photo of a baby and saying, 'His name is Daniel, and he is asking us to stop the train.' I felt like she was speaking directly to me as a father. That is why I was in front of the train."

The trial of Karol Schulkin, Glen Milner, and the other seventeen people ended that day with a "not guilty" verdict. It was another touching sight to see the court stenographer, who appeared to be about seven months pregnant, choke up as she read each individual name and said, "Not guilty, not guilty," nineteen times. Before the reading of the verdict, the judge asked for silence in the court. He wanted no outburst. However, that silence added even more power to the sight of this woman who represented the court system trying to hold back her emotions as she read the verdict.

As I sat there, I knew that the truth and the children could break down the walls that separate us. They could make us one.

• 14 •

What Do We Tell the Children?

On July 26, 1985, I stood on the beach alongside the Hood Canal and watched the USS *Henry Jackson*, America's fifth Trident submarine come "home" to Bangor. My heart was heavy. I watched children being called by excited parents to come look at the huge submarine in the water.

A small girl stooped down in front of me, fondling a shell she discovered along the shore. Her father called her away from that beauty and wonder. He asked her to look out into the canal instead, and see the ultimate weapon of destruction. For me it was as if she were being called to look at the end of the world. The picture of that small child returns to me over and over again. It is almost too much for me to bear as I realize the choice that many of us still make, calling the next generation to turn away from nature and celebrate weapons.

Three days after the *Henry Jackson* docked at Bangor, I went down to the shore of the Hood Canal with Daniel, who was then two and a half years old. Somehow I wanted to be reconciled to that place, to show reverence to the shells and rocks, and to take in the awesome beauty of it all. Daniel and I played together, throwing pebbles and enjoying their splashes. We made friends with little crabs, and we laughed as together we loved Earth and one another. The thought of the submarine was never far from me nor the knowledge that another train was loading and would be coming soon. Even as the pebbles and the water splashed, I knew that the USS *Henry Jackson* was just a mile or two south of us. It shared the same water, and was probably being prepared to be loaded with nuclear weapons transported to it by the White Train. The submarine is now part of the picture of the Hood Canal. The picture is not all beautiful, but neither are we. If we are faithful to opening ourselves up to a reality that is painful, we also open ourselves to a joy that surpasses understanding.

The times are making mystics of us, making us into what human beings are meant to be. We are meant to be part of each other, part of Earth. We are meant to hurt when one part of us hurts, to cry and grieve, meant to feel guilty if we are responsible for another's pain. We are meant to see and hear, to smell, touch, and taste life with all its ups and downs and to know the deep joy of what it means to be one with oceans and trees and one another.

These are the lessons we are meant to treasure and keep and pass on to the children.

• 15 •

The Gift of Community, The Óscar Romero Inn

Community is the invisible truth of our oneness
becoming visible in our lives.
—*Shelley Douglass*

I left Ground Zero in the fall of 1985 to continue my journey into nonviolence closer to my religious congregation and to Long Island, the place of my birth. What the Aboriginal people might call "my bone country." Little did I realize at that time how that move back to Long Island would bring me into close contact with Salvadoran refugees who had made their home here.

The Interfaith Nutrition Network, otherwise known as the INN, is an organization that provides shelter and food to people experiencing homelessness on Long Island. Sister Pat Kollmer, a member of my congregation, was at that time on the staff of the INN. Together we decided that if I would accept the position of coordinator of one of their facilities, we would use it to provide a place for Salvadorans to live in community with myself and Eileen McCormick, another Dominican sister.

We named our home for Salvadorans "The Óscar Romero Inn." I spent some of the happiest years of my life there among people who embraced suffering, and never gave up on their pursuit of justice. A poster of Archbishop Romero hung in our living room, a constant reminder of the price of truth and liberation.

Underneath his photo were the words: "If they kill me I will rise again in the people of El Salvador."[1]

The government did kill him. On March 24, 1980, he was shot in the heart while celebrating Mass. The previous day, March 23, he had preached at the Cathedral of San Salvador. In his homily he said to those in the military, "You are killing your own peasant brothers, and when faced with a man's order to kill, you should heed the law of God that says, 'Thou shalt not kill.' . . . In the name of God, in the name of this suffering people whose cries go up to heaven more painfully every day, I beg you, I implore you, I order you in the name of God: stop the repression!"[2] He was killed not because he asked people to take up arms, but because he ordered them as a bishop of the church to put the guns down.

I visited El Salvador shortly after another tragedy. On November 16, 1989, six Jesuit priests, their housekeeper, and her daughter were killed by the military.[3] I went to the University of Central America, where the priests had lived and were killed. I visited the chapel, and saw the same framed poster that hung in our living room on Long Island. After killing the priests, the military went into the chapel and again put a bullet through the heart of Archbishop Romero, now pictured in that poster. It was an unbelievable act, but one that showed he was for them still living. They believed they could kill him once again with another bullet to the heart. He had, as he had said, risen in the

---

1. This quote appears in various forms in translation. Jon Sobrino SJ attributes it to a March 1980 interview in the Mexican newspaper *Excelsior*, and we found the quote in its archives: "[S]e mi uccidono, risusciterò nel popolo salvadoregno" (Jon Sobrino, *Archbishop Romero: Memories and Reflections* [Maryknoll, NY: Orbis Books, 2016], 187).

2. Sobrino, *Archbishop Romero*, 198.

3. For an account of the crime and trial, see The International Commission of Jurists Staff, *A Breach of Impunity: The Trial for the Murder of Jesuits in El Salvador: Report of the Trial Observer of the International Commission of Jurists* (New York: Fordham University Press, 1992).

people of El Salvador. He was and is still alive, still asking for justice for the people.

We all lived life fully and together at the Óscar Romero Inn, taking turns cooking for our community, working at jobs with little pay, and often experiencing great health risks. We stayed always connected to El Salvador through messages of disappearances and killings. I oversaw a list of people who supported us, and contacted them each time there was a crisis. In those days before emails, cell phones, and Instagram, I asked them each to send a fax to the president of El Salvador, alerting him that many in the United States were watching as people disappeared. I asked them to demand accountability for those disappearances and deaths, and also demand that U.S. aid cease to the government of El Salvador. We painted banners and signs to carry during our protests and our visits to the Salvadoran embassy.

On one of those protests outside the embassy, we passed out leaflets to people on the street, alerting them to the latest atrocities in El Salvador and reminding them of the martyred archbishop, the Jesuit priests, the churchwomen, and the thousands of adults and children of El Salvador. We held a service where we gathered in a circle and passed around a basket of bread. Each person took some, a symbol of the community we shared.

Later, I and another person were designated to bring a basket with some of that bread to the embassy. We carried it to the office of the highest embassy official with the message of Archbishop Romero: we are all brothers and sisters, we are one. Stop the persecution. Stop killing your brothers and sisters. Before I entered, a man approached me, wearing an earpiece. I assumed he was FBI. He asked if I was going inside. I told him yes, and that I would carry the framed poster of Archbishop Romero. We would also bring a basket of bread. He informed me that he would go with us.

As usual, the embassy was crowded with Salvadoran people trying to take care of passports and visas and other documents affecting their lives. It was noisy as I entered, but upon seeing me carrying the image of Archbishop Romero, the entire place went silent. We proceeded to the office of the head of the embassy. He was small in stature and sat behind a large desk. He looked at us nervously, and he, too, reacted to the framed poster, which I propped up on a small couch in his office. He was unnerved by the photo. I thought how ironic it was that Archbishop Romero held so much power, even in death. I told this man who held a different kind of power that we came in peace with the message from the archbishop, and with the pleading of the four church-women who had been murdered and raped by the military of El Salvador.

Then we offered him the basket, and asked that he partake in this bread that symbolized the community we shared. He pulled back almost as though he thought it was a bomb, or some sort of weapon. He saw us as the enemy, and he found it difficult to believe we thought of him as a brother. We asked him to convey our message to the authorities in El Salvador. Archbishop Óscar Romero, a man who died because he told the truth and loved the people of El Salvador, had come again to ask that weapons be put down. He had risen as said he would, in the people of El Salvador.

*

In 1990 I was told that the United States had sent thousands of body bags to the Gulf. It was Advent, and we were preparing not for Christmas, but for war and death.

Some of us said we waited in that season for Christ to be born again; we were trying to birth God in dark times. Guadalupe made a piñata for the children's party, a snow person filled with candy. There was lots of joy on December 22 as we celebrated, laughed, sang, played, and presented each child with a gift. There was much light faithful to the Christmas season.

On December 7, I attended a beautiful religious service at

St. James in Setauket. It commemorated the tenth anniversary of the four North American churchwomen murdered in El Salvador. Surrounded by roses and candles, the relatives and friends of the slain women gathered together to remember and be called to imitate them. I arrived home late that night because of the long drive; it was 12:15 a.m. On my phone recorder was a message: "Hi Jeanne. This is Karol Schulkin (a friend and member of the Ground Zero Community still there beside the submarine base). I'm here at JFK airport. Just got in with a peace delegation from Baghdad."

I missed speaking to Karol that night, but I did not miss the connection. My heart was filled with hope knowing that Emmanuel, God with us, was truly present even as we asked for him to come. Our God was being born again through Ita, Maura, Jean, and Dorothy. Our hope was alive in the lives of people like Karol Schulkin and Jim and Shelley Douglass, who walked in the ways of peace.

༰

I spent four-and-a-half beautiful years at the Óscar Romero Inn, touched by the lives of so many wonderful and committed people. My life was richer and my hope stronger for having passed that way, and I will forever feel a part of the small country of El Salvador and the life of its people.

All of us have to go home to the land, home to a place where Earth is at the center, and where our own identity is inclusive of the Earth Community. I had similar feelings one day years before, when I had been part of a community that had stopped the White Train taking hydrogen bombs to the Trident submarine. On both occasions I knew we were closer to home; closer to that place where fear has been overcome and where we know true security lies. On both of those days, one standing at the border of El Salvador, the other on the tracks bordering the Trident submarine base, I knew that I had been witness to events that would change and deepen my life. Not only that, but these events would become the fabric and mosaic by which future generations could continue to believe in life and in the human spirit. It gave me great hope to know that people all over the world were weaving such fabric with their lives.

Now I was leaving the Óscar Romero Inn to begin a new chapter in my life and ministry, one surely related to the last two chapters of Trident and El Salvador—most definitely related with *going home*. I began my ministry by attending a program at Genesis Farm in Blairstown, New Jersey, called Earth Literacy. If we are honest with ourselves, we know we are (most of us) illiterate in things concerning Earth. To be illiterate about something as close to us as Earth is strange, and has a great deal to do, I think, with why we know ourselves and one another so little. To be illiterate about Earth is also, I believe, why we are so far from knowing God who is revealed in Earth so close to us, a part of us.

I continued to walk with the people from Central and South America, and I still do. One of our children, Rodolfo, from Guatemala, said it most succinctly back then in 1992. Rodolfo was at that time five years old. One morning as he entered the room of Norma, a Salvadoran woman then with her two-month-old son, Irvin, Rodolfo said, "*Como esta mi hermano?*" "How is my brother?"

Let's keep asking the question.

Emmanuel (1973)

Gentle seed
Far from mountain heights
Sinks into Earth and dies.
Fragile seed
Unlike the rock and peak
It neither climbs nor soars
But enters in
And needs some caring for.

El Salvador, Our Savior

There's a war going on
"Low intensity" they call it
It's bloody, bodies burn
Acid covers faces once holding
images of wonder, looks of passion
And youthful innocence

Here one would never know a war
was going on
Except sometimes on subway rides
You'd never know we were conducting it
The war I mean
Responsible
We go about our shopping living in illusions
Trying to believe that everything's OK

Some of us see and can't forget the war
The children and the blood
It's high intensity for us

The refugees are here each day
Insuring that our blindness not return
They help us see and feel and know the human
face of war
A gift to us, but one so painful it is easy
to refuse the gift
And choose instead to live a lie.

• 16 •

Led Back to the Land

When some of the Salvadoran women living with me at the Óscar Romero Inn told me about a campaign called "Going Home," and asked me to go to a refugee camp in Honduras to accompany the refugees home, I knew without a doubt that I would go. After all, that theme of home had run through my life for so long. How could I refuse?

I joined with about fifteen other North Americans who went to the refugee camp in Mesa Grande, Honduras, to accompany the Salvadoran people home. I remember the people boarding the buses with just little mesh bags holding what little they owned. Chickens rode on the roofs of the buses. Just as we were about to leave, we learned that the battery was missing in a tractor the refugees were taking home. The question was posed to the Salvadorans. Would they leave without the tractor? Or would they stay until the mystery was solved? A delegation went to each bus to obtain a consensus. The answer was they would wait. And wait we did. There was tension in the air, and we North Americans were asked why we participated in the delay. We told the authorities we would take direction from the Salvadorans, and would support their decisions. In just a little more than a half hour, the battery miraculously appeared back in the tractor. We were on our way home to El Salvador, and the tractor was going with us.

As we entered through the gate leaving the refugee camp behind, excitement grew. I realized what a moment this was in the life of each of the Salvadorans on that bus with me. But what will always remain in my mind and heart is what happened next, to me. As we drove out of the refugee camp I experienced a revelation. I too was a refugee. Certainly not in the same way as the Salvadorans were. But I had been disconnected from my land, separated. The Salvadorans knew they were going back to their land. That is why the tractor was so important to them. When I thought of my home in the United States, land was not a part of my consciousness. I had been disconnected from it.

I was accompanying the Salvadorans home to their land. But they were accompanying me back to find a land that I had never known.

• 17 •

Elderberries:
In Search of Truth

Earth is in need of so many things these days. One of these, I believe, is the active presence of elders. At the age of 84 I find myself not winding down, not ready to retire and take a cruise somewhere. I am awake and alive to the times I am living in, knowing that I was born into these times with something only I can give by being who I truly am.

Being who I truly am is a life-long journey of disconnecting from a culture that sees me and everyone around me as a consumer, one ready to compete, to go to war with anyone who threatens the lifestyle I have become accustomed to. It is a culture disconnected from Earth and her wisdom, focused on the individual human. There is a lot of leaving and grieving to be the person who I really am in such a culture. But there is also a great deal of joy.

Thomas Berry, a Passionist priest, knew at a very early age that what was good for the meadow was good, and what was bad for the meadow was bad. He has had a tremendous impact on my life, and his book *Dream of the Earth* still guides me when I lose my way. He gave me the deep understanding that we as humans are the Universe conscious of itself. We are connected to everything that is, and that has made all the difference. Thomas told us that we are at a crossroad, a time to choose our direction. One road leads to the Ecozoic, a time when the human and natural world will go into the future together in a mutually enhancing way. The other road leads to the Technozoic, believing that technology will solve all our problems.

᷄

Many years ago I became part of a group of women dedicated to understanding and living out their lives following the teachings of Thomas Berry. They named themselves after a beautiful berry—Elderberries—since they were both elders and followers of Berry. They asked me to facilitate a retreat for them each year in Vermont. We spent time looking at and trying to comprehend the new teachings from the scientist Brian Swimme, who taught and wrote with Berry and others such as Matthew Fox and Mary Evelyn Tucker, and who reflected on what this New Cosmology meant in our lives. I can remember us Elderberries spending hours watching the video series *Canticle to the Cosmos*, replaying sections of it over and over while trying to grasp the truth of it all. We prayed, laughed, told stories, and prepared delicious meals together as we studied amid the beauty of Vermont.

We learned that Earth is in need of elders who believe that the Ecozoic is still possible. It would seem, however, that all the evidence is leading us to believe that the Technozoic is taking over.

The vision of the Ecozoic has been leading me since 1992 when I studied at Genesis Farm with Miriam MacGillis, who incorporated the work of Thomas Berry into all of her endeavors. My time at Genesis Farm and my immersion in Thomas Berry's thought synthesized and connected for me all the threads of my personal journey. They led me to that moment when I realized that I had to come home to the place where I was born and had lived for most of my life. I had to come home to Long Island and plant the seeds of the Ecozoic. It was here on Long Island that Homecoming Farm was born, at the motherhouse of the Amityville Dominicans. It is a CSA (a community-supported

Sister Jeanne Clark at Homecoming Farm.
Credit: Meiling Sandy Ku, used with permission.

agricultural project) that is committed to the understanding that the human and natural world are one sacred community of life. We attempt to live that belief by connecting adults, teenagers, and children to the land, to seeds and soil, worms and bees, butterflies and insects of all kind, and discover together that we are all one sacred community of life.

As fires and floods rage around us and we wonder what the future holds, I grieve the loss of so much beauty, so much life. I hold on to all the life at Homecoming Farm and our attempts to give to the next generation a spirituality based in Earth and her wisdom. I give thanks to all the Elderberries; those living and still awestruck by the new discoveries in science and those who have left us to discover even more awesome realities. I now see the fabric of my life as a beautiful tapestry connected to stars and galaxies, to sun and moon, and all creatures of Earth. I am traveling together with all of creation, planting seeds of the Ecozoic. So many have already lost their habitat and gone extinct; the human too is threatened with that possibility. Although I grieve the loss and know the future we have created for the young holds much pain and chaos, I continue with others planting seeds of the Ecozoic and embracing Earth with all her wisdom. How far in do I want to go? Thank God for truth and love and the way that they allure us to continue on. They call us to go all the way in.

• 18 •

Why I Love Being with Children

Of all the grades I've taught, first grade was my favorite. Imagination can be so alive in children; they are present to the moment, shutting out all else but what is right before them. When I'm with children I can talk to trees and animals can dance and jump and throw caution to the wind. I can step in puddles or in mud without the worry of getting dirty. I can say what's on my mind and can cry without holding back.

The abuse of children seems to touch us more than any other. Wartime images of harm repel us more when it is children who are bloody or without limbs. It was the photo of the little girl in Vietnam in 1972 running naked as she was burned by napalm that touched the world and brought us to our senses for a moment. We want to protect the young, to preserve their innocence. That photo and its reality were disturbing.

The image of the little girl with the seashell I spoke about while I was waiting for the *Henry Jackson*, America's fifth Trident submarine, stays with me. I have never forgotten how she was so taken by a beautiful shell she had found on the shore. Instead she was called away by her father from that discovery to look at and celebrate a weapon that could destroy the world as we know it. This image tells the story of our culture and what we value. We spend trillions of dollars on weapons of war while so many children go hungry and experience an inferior education. What is it we are teaching our children to see, to connect to, to love? What is it we value and want to pass on to our children?

My goddaughter, Elizabeth, and her husband, John, gave birth to twin boys, John and James, nine years ago. I love to be with them and watch them grow. Though coming from the same womb, the same parents, and the same home, they are so different, each unique in his likes and things that attract. John always wants to figure out how things work. He likes to build and create things. He loves outer space and astronauts.

I remember James, who at the age of three and a half was going through a box of figurines while I sat eating breakfast at his house after an overnight stay. He came and placed a gift at my plate, one of his figurines. It was a ninja with a sword, ready for battle. I looked at James and told him that it was not one of my favorites. I shared with him why I didn't like swords, and battling other people. I explained to him that swords cut and hurt and make others cry. He quickly took the ninja back and threw him in the box with all the other characters. Then he searched and found one he thought might please me. He came to me again and placed Minnie Mouse next to my plate.

I smiled warmly and thanked him for this gift. "I like her! She's happy, and she makes me smile, too."

It seems like such a little thing, and unimportant, but children notice what we like, what captures our attention.

Years later James came to me again. I think he hoped that I had changed my mind.

"I know you don't like guns," he said to me. "But how about swords?"

I went through my routine again. "I know that toy swords don't hurt, but real ones cut and people bleed."

"How about cannons?"

He somehow didn't want to let the weapons go, but what I liked mattered to him, so he continued to try to convince me. I think he had in mind a toy that loaded a ball and shot it out like a cannon.

"Oh, cannons hurt a lot of people, not just one. You shoot the weapon, and you may not see the people, but when it lands it hurts a lot of people."

James got the message that I didn't like hurting people, even people I didn't know or couldn't see. He seemed satisfied that I had answered all his questions.

A year or two later I was speaking on the phone with James, and he told me, "Auntie Jeanne, I got a toy favor at a birthday party, but I don't think you are going to like it."

"Well, I'll be seeing you soon. You can show it to me when I visit next week."

When I drove up to the house, James was playing on the lawn with the biggest water gun I had ever seen. He came to the car and waited for me to comment.

"It only shoots water, and doesn't hurt anyone," he said.

"I know it doesn't hurt when you shoot water, James. But I just wish it were in the shape of a tomato or a carrot, and not a gun."

He smiled and seemed to understand. James knows I don't like guns.

As I write this, four teenagers were shot last week in Detroit, Michigan, as they attended school. They were killed by a fifteen-year-old boy who had ready access to a weapon. Judging from some of his posts on social media, it became apparent that he was enamored with a gun his father bought just days before the shooting.

Also this week in Congress, legislators introduced a bill to fund the military budget. It passed in the House of Representatives with bipartisan support. We cannot garner bipartisan support to help families who struggle or to reduce the overwhelming stress of going into debt to attain a college degree. We cannot seem to become united around a plan to address all the issues of climate disruption or the loss of biodiversity. The only thing that seems to unite the Congress of the United States is our need for more money for weapons, for what we call our defense.

We continue to show by our actions that when there is a choice between Earth and her beauty and wisdom, or weapons, war, and destruction, we choose weapons. We still tell our children through our choices as a nation that we love weapons more than life itself. We love weapons more than we love children. If there was ever a time when the changing of the mind and consciousness of the human was more needed, it is now. The stakes are so very, very high if our minds do not change.

It is time, as we watch the fires burn, the floods overwhelm, and the glaciers melt, to redefine security.

• 19 •

A Different Way of Seeing

I was born on Long Island and have lived here for most of my life, but until the early 1990s I really didn't know Long Island at all. In a very real way I didn't know myself.

The people of El Salvador had led me back to the land in the late 1980s, when I attempted to go home with them from the refugee camp in Honduras. Little did I realize then that in helping them to go home, I was being led home. This was not only to the land but to an understanding of myself that would change my life. It would connect me in a very deep way to the ocean, the sun, to the fish and birds, and all the creatures of Earth. I would know myself as the Earth and the Universe, conscious of itself with the powers of the Universe housed within me. I would experience a way of belonging I could never have imagined.

I came home to Long Island in 1992 after a profound experience of exploration at Genesis Farm with Miriam MacGillis and the teaching of Thomas Berry. I needed companions who would understand this new way of seeing I had discovered, and who would help me to deepen that understanding and share this great mystery with others.

This discovery was at the heart of Homecoming Farm. It began in 1996 on an acre and a half of land in Amityville, Long Island, at the motherhouse of the Sisters of Saint Dominic. In the beginning the farm was called Sophia Garden. We named it after both Sister Sophia, who loved the land, children, and the poor, and also Sophia, the feminine face of God, the name for wisdom in the Old Testament. I knew then that Earth held the wisdom we craved in these difficult times. We all needed to connect to Earth and discover her wisdom. I wanted to connect people to this small parcel of land here on Long Island, to the soil and microbes hidden beneath, and to all the life waiting to be discovered. I especially wanted the children to know a different way of seeing and connecting to life, to give them the depth of a spirituality connected to Earth that they would need to face the future we were leaving them.

I found two companions to begin my journey in the educational area of the farm. They were companions who—like me—knew that the farm was about much more than vegetables. Of course, the organic growing was a big part of it. It would aid in the health of people, the soil, and the water system, and would be the place of learning. But the deeper heart of Sophia Garden (later Homecoming Farm) and its vision was devoted to a new way of seeing. One particular quote of Thomas Berry summed up for us the kernel of a truth hidden from us by a culture that makes everything an object, even the children themselves. Thomas told us "The Universe is a communion of subjects, not a collection of objects."[1] To come to the farm is to experience everything as a subject, the soil, the seeds, worms, ants, and bees, the birds and plants, the flowers and all humans, all subjects connected to one another as one whole. They are a communion of subjects woven together as the Universe, always changing, evolving, expanding, and one. The children would learn Thomas Berry's wisdom that there is no such thing as the human community, only the life community of which the human is a part. The ants, worms, bees, flowers, and birds and all the creatures of Earth are one community of life. We are

---

1. Thomas Berry, *Evening Thoughts: Reflecting on Earth as Sacred Community*, ed. Mary Evelyn Tucker (San Francisco: Sierra Club Books, 2006), 17-18.

never alone, never separate, never isolated, only together at each moment, always in communion.

Imagine if we could all begin to see this way, to see reality as it is, to see the truth. We believed it was possible and so we began.

～

Sister Joyce Hummel and Tom Stock joined me in this new venture of education—Joyce with her love and knowledge of science, and Tom, who knew every inch of Long Island as the naturalist he is. They taught me so much, since like most folks living on Long Island I knew very little about its natural life. I was Earth illiterate, but had somehow been given this vision coming from science, challenging me to begin in spite of it.

And so Joyce and Tom joined me to develop programs for those children who would come to the farm and fall in love with life. And in the process, the three of us would be led by those children, and the tiny creatures we now saw as members of the community. We were led deeper and deeper into the truth. These times were making mystics of us all.

• 20 •

I Don't Believe It! Teaching Composting to Kids

An eight-year-old girl with her hands on her hips exclaimed in a loud voice, "I don't believe it!" She had just discovered the mystery, magic, and miracle of composting.

Teaching about composting to little children became one of my favorite lessons at the farm. Compost teaches so many truths, the central one being that life changes, things decay and die, nothing stays the same (unless, of course, it is artificial), and it is good. Earth creates new life from decay and death. What is seen by some as garbage can, when given back to Earth, become new life for the soil.

I would meet with a small group of six- to eight-year-olds in a gazebo bordering the farm. It was a very intimate circle where all of us could hear each other and see one another's beautiful faces. I came prepared with my little bucket of what I called "treasures." The children at first could not see what was in my bucket, and so they were very interested when I told them it contained treasures. I imagined that many of them thought of candy or cookies, or maybe something even more alluring. I passed the bucket around for each individual child to see.

Then their noses turned up, and a frown came to each face. They looked up at me as if maybe I had lost my mind. The bucket returned to me and I asked a question.

74

"Looks like you would not call the contents of my bucket treasures. What would you call it?"

"Garbage!" was the loud response.

"Well, let's see what's really in here."

I went on to catalogue the contents of the bucket. We found a tea bag, the end of a head of lettuce, the ends of carrots and celery, some coffee grinds from breakfast, and other contents from the compost bucket, which sits on my kitchen sink and gathers all the scraps while I'm making supper.

"Today we are going to learn how Earth in her wisdom knows how to change these little scraps we call garbage into something beautiful," I said.

Then I suggested an activity. "Let's go to the farm and look at some piles the farmer has out there. Who would like to carry the bucket? We are going to give its contents to Earth as a gift to her for all she has given us this season."

The children followed me, still a bit incredulous, but curious.

What followed was a tour of three piles the farmer had at the edge of the property. One was in process, and we could see scraps of food, some grass, and parts of plants still sitting on top, waiting to be turned.

"Let's give our gift to Earth right here," I said. "Let's throw it on the pile and learn what happens to it."

The second pile was further on. It had been turned a few times. "You see all the things the farmer placed on the pile are now being turned over and over. The farmer has added grass and horse manure, and has turned it over and over and over again. It gets pretty hot as it is turned and turned."

Then we went to the third pile. "Now let's see how that one looks. This pile is what we call 'finished.' All the scraps have disappeared. It was turned and turned, and now what does it look like?"

"I don't believe it!" a little girl shouted. "It turned into soil."

Well, almost. What is produced in composting is not actually soil, but humus, which nourishes the soil. Topsoil actually takes Earth hundreds of years to produce. But I didn't want to interrupt the joy being expressed by becoming too technical with the children. Teaching the difference between humus and soil could be left for another day.

After this lesson, we gathered at a picnic table to eat our lunch, and we talked about how we could give any leftovers to the compost pile. One little girl came and asked me to give her small plastic bottle that had held juice back to Earth.

"Oh we won't be able to give this to the compost pile," I told her. "This is manufactured by humans. Earth doesn't know what to do with this. It won't break down in the compost. That's why we should not use much plastic, and we should ask the people who make these juice containers to use paper instead."

We finished our lunch and talked about coming back tomorrow to learn more about Earth.

"If you would like," I said, "you could bring some scraps from home to give to Earth tomorrow."

The next day as the children arrived, I noticed many of them with little bags of vegetable scraps as gifts for Earth. One mother stopped to tell me what had happened in her home. That morning her husband was eating a banana at breakfast. He began to toss the skin into the trash.

"Oh no," his daughter cried out. "Don't do that. That's not garbage. Earth knows how to change that into soil. I will bring it to the farm."

I was hoping these were life lessons that would continue on in these children's worlds. Back then there was not as much reinforcement in our culture for learning from Earth and acknowledging her wisdom. But for us at Sophia Garden, these days were healing and beautiful. They held the promise of a different way of seeing. By seeing differently we saw miracles all around us.

• 21 •

A Sense of Place

Wendell Berry has said, "If you don't know where you are, you don't know who you are."[1] Knowing where we are is so important. As a culture we have lost this sense of place. We really don't know where we are. Very few people who live on Long Island carry a true understanding that they are on an actual island. We live among shopping centers and highways where we race back and forth, not knowing or even aware of the soil around us or the life of the trees or animals, the insects who inhabit this island with us. Most of us probably do not know when the osprey leaves or returns to Long Island, or the names and habits of the birds, or the abundant life in the Atlantic Ocean and Long Island Sound. And we have no awareness or experience that we live in the Milky Way and on Earth as our home. I was once one of these people. I grew up without a sense of place and a true knowledge of who I am.

Sister Joyce Hummel, Tom Stock, and I were so happy doing programs for children and connecting them to all the life at Sophia Garden, and later Homecoming Farm. I was aware that there were so many children in parts of Long Island that did not

---

1. Mary Modeen and Iain Biggs point out in *Creative Engagements with Ecologies of Place: Geopoetics, Deep Mapping and Slow Residencies* (London: Routledge 2020), 221n16, that Wallace Stegner attributed the quote to Wendell Berry, but it seems have originated in Ralph Ellison's novel *Invisible Man* (New York: Random House, 1952), 562.

have the opportunity to join our programs and were living in places surrounded by cement with little access to nature. The Sisters of St. Dominic of Amityville generously provided us with a grant that enabled us to go into schools staffed by the Dominican Sisters in Brooklyn. We chose three schools and developed a two-year program for each school, which included lessons in the classrooms of two grades, teacher workshops so the teachers would have a sense of what the children were learning, and an assembly each year for the entire school where the children would share in a creative way some of the lessons they had learned. Each year, both classes came to the farm, where Earth herself would capture the imagination and heart of every child. It was during one of these trips to the farm that I heard words I never would have imagined from a child growing up in Brooklyn. While boarding the bus to go back to school I heard one of the eighth-grade boys say, "I think I would like to be a farmer."

There are so many stories to tell about the years we spent in the schools in Brooklyn. Sister Joyce and I spent a good deal of time teaching about watersheds, and how important it was to know how your watershed is affected by what humans do on the land. In order to get an idea of the children's understanding of water, I asked one morning if some of the children could share their experience. Of course, we all had the experience of water coming out of the tap in the sink, but what other experience of water did the children have? None of the children shared any experience of the ocean, even though it was no more than two miles from their school. Some of them I am sure had been to a beach at some point, but in their daily living their experience of any body of water was absent. Their only daily contact with water other than from the tap was puddles. These were children living on an island surrounded by water, but whose living situation surrounded by cement had robbed them of really knowing where they lived.

If Joyce, Tom, and I could help expand their knowledge of

where they lived, perhaps they, too, could learn and experience a new way of seeing and of knowing who they really were. They lived not only on this small patch of cement, but on Earth and in the Universe. They would learn that there were more than pigeons, mice, rats, and squirrels here on Long Island where they lived. They were amazed when they learned that just a few miles from them there were whales swimming far out in the Atlantic Ocean, and so many varieties of birds who passed through as they migrated to other places. These were not fantasies. This was life just a few miles away.

Joyce, Tom, and I attempted to bring to these children a new awareness of where they lived. By sharing with them the New Story coming to us through science, they gained a new understanding of who they really were. Their identity was not in being consumers. They came from the stars, and all the elements in their bodies were first in stars. They were not alone, and they were not just individuals. Yes, they themselves were unique, and they had gifts to give that no others could give. But they were one with all creation, connected to everything that lived. Their home was here in Brooklyn on Long Island, but also on the Earth and in the Universe. We were learning together to embrace this new way of seeing, of becoming different people. Perhaps Earth has a chance for healing, for regeneration. And if she cannot heal, at least she will be loved and cherished, and all her disappearing species will be grieved.

We were coming home to our place and experiencing a way of belonging we had never known before.

Solar Energy

I sat beside the Great South Bay reading chapter 5 in Brian Swimme's book *Hidden Heart of the Cosmos*. The sun was beaming down, the water receiving its loving caress. This poem came to me.

Tears come when I become aware.
Amazing truth breaks in
reminding me again of my
connection to all others in a stream of energy
not earned or bought.

Each day enough, no running out.
This giant star gives of itself and energizes me.
Abundance given equally to all.

A sacrifice is asked
To give away a part of me in creative acts of love.
Communion

The seagulls flying just above the water
Their wings propelled by energy we share.
They soar and play, they hunt for
food existing by the very energy allowing them to fly.
I breathe the air and say a prayer of gratitude.
Communion

The world around me goes about its daily tasks
To work, to buy, to sell.
I yearn that all might know the simple truth
So clear yet veiled and needing time and space
to see and understand.

A world of energy and love is dawning
A great turning taking place.
The seagulls and the water, the fish unseen below
all tell the story.
The sun graces all of us.
Even in the darkness the sacredness of life exists
And energy abounds

She Looked at Me

The seagull looked at me.
We met eye to eye
Don't know what she sees.
Is it me?

I see her.
How she loves the water
So do I.

We came here to the Great South Bay
To connect. To be nourished.
To feel the breeze, to smell the salt
To know something of our beginnings.

The water, a mysterious ancestor
Calling us to stop and know the deep mystery.
A oneness, a communion of all that is different
And in so many ways the same.

She flies away.

I am reminded that she can fly.
Coming from a common source
We travel together.
She in the air
Me on the ground
United in the same Earthly home
Traveling at great speed.

We are cosmic she and I
She the Universe in the form of a bird
I in the form of a human.

Awestruck I give thanks
For this moment in time.

• 22 •

Being with Children at the Farm

I love introducing children to ways of seeing that are new to them, and wonder filled. Earth and soil have so much wisdom to share with children. They give them an appreciation of intelligence and a way of living and working as a community we previously thought was reserved only for humans. Children actually find out that ants and bees work better as a community than many humans, and they do a great deal more for Earth's life.

When they come to the farm, the children turn off the noise and advertisements bombarding them with messages of things they supposedly need in order to be happy. They listen instead to the wind in the trees, the flowers, plants, and insects who make their home here. They become intimate with a place, and their community grows and expands to include the stars and galaxies and all the creatures of Earth. It feels like paradise at times.

Their visits at the farm are limited, and most of their days, weeks, and months are filled with other activities: school and soccer, dance and baseball. They are always on the move, usually rushing from one thing to another with little time to just be still with nothing to do. And if by chance time like this makes itself available, the first thing they experience is boredom. "I'm bored," we often hear them say. Boredom marks a perfect time to turn to phones and iPads, where they take in anything being offered to them. As they grow they accumulate

Homecoming Farm. Photo by James Jarosz.

"friends" online, but hardly know themselves, the friend that lives within them.

I knew the children often were exhausted, but they didn't even know it themselves. I wanted to give them space and time to slow down and connect with another whole world inside of them.

I decided one day to take a chance and experiment with a little space I called "Quiet Time." Because the children were between six and eight years old, I thought the time needed to be short. I think I was mistaken.

I gathered the children in a small circle and asked them if they ever spent time outside just sitting without a book or radio or phone. "Just you."

They looked at me with puzzled faces. I could tell the question was unimaginable and the negative answer was obvious.

And so I went on with my experiment. "Today we are going to go out alone and sit for a short period of time, just listening. We can choose anywhere we like . . . alongside the farm, under those big Norway maple trees, or maybe you would prefer a place in the sun. You might be able to hear the wind or other voices on the farm. You can—if you want to—feel the grass.

Since we spray no chemicals, you might even want to taste it, or taste a leaf that has fallen. You might want to smell the grass and leaves. Don't forget the sky and clouds. You can look up and see the vastness of your space. And then I want you to listen to see if you can hear a tiny voice inside you. It is yourself, and if you remain very still and quiet you can hear yourself speak to you. Sometimes yourself is happy, and sometimes sad. Ask yourself how you are feeling today. Listen to the birds that are singing, and if you are sad they will listen and be with you. So will the trees and the wind. You might, if you look carefully, see a passing butterfly or bee. You can say hello. Earth loves spending time with you.

"So now take your small blanket and find a place. Remember it is not time to talk to one another. It is time to be alone. Just you and this place together."

My experiment took place within a week-long day program at the farm. The next day, as the children arrived, a little eight-year-old girl ran up to me to ask, "Sister, are we going to have Quiet Time again?"

"Yes if you would like."

"Can it be longer?"

We gathered together after each period of "Quiet Time." We were growing and loving one another and this place. And we were listening to the seed of who we each were, so unique and special.

Thomas Berry, whose teachings are at the heart of Homecoming Farm, taught me about the three principles of the Universe: interiority or subjectivity, differentiation, and communion. My time with the children on that lovely day at the farm taught them that they are a subject living among other subjects like trees and butterflies.

We are not here to use things or places or people. We are here as subjects to be in relationship to all that is. It is a beautiful way to live. It is a way of living in paradise.

The children learned from the quiet and stillness, and discovered the miracle of their inner lives. My hope is that they will continue to communicate with that life and discover the unique gift they are. They are the Universe conscious of itself, each one of them different, each one with life emerging from within as subject. Each one is embedded in Earth and living in communion with all the others, even with the microbes in the soil, invisible and giving life without asking anything in return.

Oh, how I yearn that each one of these precious children will be led to discover over and over again this wondrous truth. In the world of chaos and violence that surrounds them, may we prepare them by giving them a vision of another world where all is one. That world exists and is waiting for us to lift the veil and enter in. The next generation is in need of elders who know this other world exists.

· 23 ·

Food Is at the Heart
of Our Transformation

I was reminded once again as I prepared the evening meal yesterday that food is at the heart of our transformation. I had decided to roast all the vegetables that called to me from their drawer in the refrigerator, as some showed signs of heading to the compost. As I took my knife and started cutting, I was taken with the beauty of the different colors and shapes. There were vibrant red, yellow, orange, and green peppers, and small round potatoes that had been harvested from our farm two weeks earlier. They were so abundant that there were still many, even after enjoying a meal with them last week. The carrots would have been tossed by those who shop in supermarkets and want only perfect looking veggies. This crop of carrots did not pass the good-looking test. They were of all different shapes and sizes, and had black marks on their skin. Usually I would not peel them since there is nutrition in their skin, but I peeled these and cut them all into the same size. Magically, their appearance now rivaled the beauty of the peppers. The onions, white and beautiful, added another color to the meal. Since some of the small tomatoes were in need of saving, I decided to add them to the roasting tray.

I thought of Thomas Berry, who in his brilliance gave us the three principles at the heart of the Universe: differentiation, subjectivity, and communion.[1]

---

1. Thomas Berry, *Evening Thoughts: Reflecting on Earth as Sacred Com-*

And here they were gathered together on the tray, ready to go into the oven for roasting. Just one color or shape or taste would not be as delicious or appealing. Earth gives us an abundance of colors, shapes, and tastes and asks us in our creativity to add more and more variety, and to appreciate and celebrate not sameness but difference. And each of these wonderful vegetables was a subject, not an object. Each began as a tiny seed that miraculously knew it was the seed of a carrot, or potato, or pepper. Their ancestry went back thousands of years. They were in deep relationship to the sun and the water that nurtured them and gifted them with life. And they were waiting to share their life with us as we ate a meal and joined in a communion so deep that the vegetables became us, became part of our bones and muscles, our brain.

As I prepared our meal yesterday I thought about all of us who struggle to find meaning in this world that seems to be spiraling out of control. We are being asked to face the reality that we humans are—by the very lives we are living—destroying so much of life. So many of us ask, "What can I do?" In my own life I have come to the conclusion that the most important thing is to align my life with the life of the Universe expressed in these three principles of differentiation, subjectivity, and communion. It might seem simplistic to say, but a very important thing to do is rooted in what all of us do every day more than once. We eat.

But how we grow the food we eat makes all the difference on whether Earth is nourished and celebrated or on the other hand Earth's life is diminished and destroyed.

The seed of Homecoming Farm that began in 1996 as Sophia Garden was rooted in the wisdom of Earth, who led us into deeper understandings of not only how to grow vegetables, herbs, and flowers, but to get glimpses of how to live in align-

---

munity, ed. Mary Evelyn Tucker (San Francisco: Sierra Club Books, 2006), 145.

ment with the Universe. It has not been an easy journey. We try to live in unity with the Universe by the way we grow food, but perhaps the greatest obstacle has been an extractive economy that does not support relationships and communion. It is an economy based on consuming, and on seeing land and food as objects.

The food industry is just that, an industry. It sees land, seeds, plants, and animals as objects to be used by humans. They are commodities that enrich not our bodies but the pockets of those who see food not as nourishment but as a means of control and making money. In this industry land is stressed beyond limits, soil pumped with chemicals destroying all the life within it, killing the microbes that although unseen are the real farmers providing us with food. This industry changes the DNA of tomatoes, potatoes, corn, and other vegetables through the use of GMOs, changing a memory that has existed in their seeds through millennia. How can we call the product of this industry food? It is a desecration and out of alignment with a Universe who for billions of years has given us all that we need to flourish and grow. And if this desecration were not enough, the farm workers who labor so hard in the chemically laden fields and without whom this industry would grind to a halt are paid subsistence salaries, making their lives miserable.

Our government supports this industry, subsidizes it. Meanwhile, farmers on small farms who are trying to regenerate the soil and help to heal Earth as she labors to preserve life are left on their own, struggling to survive.

～

In 2010, as Elizabeth Keihm took the position of director of Homecoming Farm, she faced the obstacle of economic insecurity. It called forth all the creativity within her. Because of her past history as florist and event planner, she provided us with beautiful fundraising events in an effort to balance our budget and keep the farm in operation. This obstacle is faced by all small farms not only here on Long Island but throughout the country. Many farmers have to hold down two or more jobs, and it is the reason why many small farms don't make it.

We were so fortunate that Don Cimato found his way to Homecoming Farm as our farmer. In Don we found a person who lives in the area and has been committed to the farm long-term. He is loved by the apprentices and interns who learn from him, and by the shareholders at the farm who appreciate his hard work and dedication in growing delicious and healthy food that they share with their families.

As spring approaches, Don can be found in the greenhouse, one of his favorite places. There he relates to the seeds, now beginning to sprout as tiny seedlings, which he nourishes with love. He also has a gift for researching and finding ways to adapt to the diseases and pests that arrive due to climate change. The squash vine borer, a type of destructive moth, has impacted our production of both summer and winter squash.

Don now grows summer squash within a time window when the squash vine borer is not active. In the past we grew several varieties of winter squash that are now impossible to grow. However, Don did his research and found that butternut squash stems are small and tight and are not conducive to the borer's growth in the plant. And so Don uses butternut squash seeds from around the world. They vary in size and subtleties of taste, so we can still have winter squash for distribution.

In the past we also grew early, middle, and late varieties of potatoes, but our potato crop is quite vulnerable to wireworm. Don solved the problem by growing only the early variety of potato, so that they are not in the ground long enough for the wireworm to get access. He also grows them in boxes filled with soil to alleviate the problem. As you can see, a good farmer is always finding ways to adapt and discover new ways of growing food without too much loss. As we look into the future with all the disruption connected with climate change, we know that Don's gifts will be more and more needed.

All of us at Homecoming Farm have learned to appreciate farmers who love what they do. It includes honoring the rhythm of the seasons, the sacredness of seed and soil, and using regenerative growing methods, all while working with the impacts of weather, pests, and disease in a time of climate change. In the spirit of the CSA movement, it is not just about getting food for our tables, but "knowing the face of the farmer." And we do.

So many of us in all walks of life are trying to survive these days. It is exhausting. Here at Homecoming Farm it is our vision that keeps us going. It draws on all the creativity within us to try to overcome this obstacle by creating the beginnings of a new economy. In 1996 we thought it would be possible through the CSA model. In this model, families support the farmer by buying a share of the produce, giving the farmer a ready-made market. CSA members are shareholders who provide economic support. We have been a CSA for twenty-five years, and this model has given us a beautiful community of people who love the farm and have been connected to Earth in ways that supermarkets cannot provide. We have become a community of people who know their farmer, who know the place where their food grows, and who have come to know one another in a community formed around food. If the shareholders would pay the cost of what it really costs to grow organic food, then the farm could survive. However most of the shareholders of Homecoming Farm are middle-class folks who in the current economy are trying to survive as families.

The story continues as we reject a consumer model of food and follow our desire to align ourselves with the life of the Universe. If we understand the Story of the Universe and how life and complexity have emerged through billions of years, we learn that extraction is not the way. We learn that the growth and complexity of life come out of relationship and cooperation, which regenerate life. When we are in relationship and cooperate with the microbes, earthworms, pollinators, and all the life in the soil, abundance is the result, not depletion. We know we are not alone in this struggle, but united with people around the globe who attempt to live in what Thomas Berry would call a "mutually enhancing way" with Earth.[2]

It is the way of the Universe that obstacles, when faced, can be the source of moving forward to greater life. Perhaps it is because obstacles can be the means of enabling our imagination to come alive and expand. Earth today depends on the life-giving gift of human imagination. I am reminded as I write this of Einstein's statement that hangs from the wall in the office of Homecoming Farm: "Imagination is more important than knowledge."[3]

Elizabeth has been gifted with an abundance of imagination. Since we lacked money in order to provide many of the things needed at the farm, she found a way to have all of our infrastructure built by teenagers. Eagle Scouts are always looking for projects, and Homecoming Farm always has things needing to be built. It was a perfect marriage. Of course, it never would have worked without Elizabeth's imagination, patience, and perseverance. She has worked with well over fifty Eagle Scouts as well as several Gold Award Girl Scouts who came to the farm looking for a project. She provides them with creative ideas of what they might do and stays with them through all stages of development through completion. She has come to know their parents and supporters who accompany them to the farm as they complete their projects, and she has attended each of their ceremonies to congratulate them on their success. Because of their efforts, Homecoming Farm has been gifted with beautiful structures that would have otherwise cost tens of thousands of dollars. The

---

2. Berry, *Evening Thoughts*, 22.

3. Albert Einstein with George Bernard Shaw, *Albert Einstein on Cosmic Religion and Other Opinions and Aphorisms* (Mineola, NY: Dover Publications, 2009 [originally published 1931]), 97.

Scouts built a gazebo that is wheelchair accessible. Now people who would not have ever been able to walk onto the farm can sit and gaze at the beauty of the plants and flowers, observe the working of the farmer, apprentice, and interns, and feel a part of it all. One of the Scouts had the idea of creating a labyrinth where people could walk to become more mindful. That labyrinth sits in the grass in front of the gazebo. It is surrounded by flowers, and it invites folks to come and be for a while.

They also added permanent fencing made from cedar, allowing peas and other climbing vegetables to grow. Our welcome shed provides members of the farm with gloves and tools, along with instructions of work needing to be done. The washing station is a central place of gathering, providing a place where vegetables can be washed without creating mud. Because of its overhang protection, it is a place to sort the harvested vegetables, and for workers to sit and rest awhile, protected from the sun.

Our apiary began as a Girl Scout project with two beehives. The young woman who took on the project became the recipient of the Girl Scout Gold Award, and she went on to study environmental science and entomology, focusing on pollinators in New York State.[4] This project allows us to protect the pollinators who are so necessary to our farm. The bees produce both pollen and nectar in a safe, chemical-free environment and also produce delicious honey, which makes the project self-supporting. When two hives were no longer enough, we added to the apiary. Another Eagle Scout project was born: an Eagle Scout enlarged our apiary, so that we are now up to eleven hives. This project is indicative of what happens at Homecoming Farm; it impacted the health of the pollinators we need for our food production, protecting the lives of honeybees, while enhancing the futures of two individual teenagers. It continues to enable us to welcome

---

4. For more about her accomplishment, see the website for the Girl Scouts of Nassau and Suffolk Counties, www.gsnc.org.

committed beekeepers, and ensures the future of our farm. In a sense, the entire Earth community finds a home at Homecoming Farm. The Honey House and Insect Hotel are located in a place we lovingly call "The Insect Sanctuary," and on and on and on. The creativity from these partnerships is boundless.

Not having enough money for infrastructure was an obstacle we faced. Little did we know that because of Elizabeth's imagination and creativity, and that of these young people, we would not only have all our infrastructure built but gain creativity and community in the process.

↝

We still struggle with providing an economy that would allow the farm to flourish and go into the future. We are so grateful to Elizabeth for all she is and all she has given of herself to protect the life of Homecoming Farm. We trust that the seeds we have planted will spread, knowing that food is at the heart of our transformation.

When Peacemaking Divides

My father was a New York City detective, working at what he called "the job." He knew what the DC jail was like, so when my friend Margaret told him about my arrest and that I had been taken there, he said, "I think she has lost her mind."

In some way he was right. I had lost the mind I had, and I had taken on another. My mistake, which led to my father's pain, was that I did not communicate that change of mind to him, and so it was a shock. Seeing the truth of things differently can cause divisions in a relationship. Loving the one who sees differently and trying to listen and understand are important if that division is to be made whole. This I am sure we all know is a part of all of our lives and is at the heart of not only my personal journey in nonviolence but is at the heart of our global life together.

My father always taught me to tell the truth. He also modeled for me a life of caring about others, of accepting the differences in people. He was a man of compassion, not judgment. He was also a storyteller, and all the stories were either related to "the job" or else to the way he grew up. Instead of getting new shoes, he went to the shoemaker to ask if anyone had left shoes behind. His mother bought old bread, soaked it, and put it in the oven to make it taste fresh. He worked from a very young age. When he and his brother, Charlie, were teenagers, they lived at the YMCA after their mother died at forty-two.

In our family you could observe our smiling faces when my father began one of these stories we had heard before. We knew he loved "the job," and it was very much a part of our lives. I always remember how he came home from work each night. Before he took off his coat and hat, he reached to his side, opened a cabinet drawer, put something inside it, and closed and locked the drawer. I never saw his gun, but I knew that he locked it up each time before taking off his coat. We also knew the partners he had on the job, and they felt almost like family to us. As I grew, I understood that my father's life depended on his partner. It was a relationship based on trust.

In many Irish families when I was growing up, the New York City Police Department was a part of the family, similar to the parish church. It was a piece of our identity, and things were very clear. There was right and wrong. There were those who obeyed the law and those who broke the law. There were the good and the bad. As a child, I grew up believing that since my father was such a good man, that all police were good, and the people they put in jail were bad. Since I never knew anyone who had gone to jail, it was easy to believe in the sides, the good and the bad. And, of course, in my mind I stood on the side of good. I tried my best to obey all the laws and the Ten Commandments, and if I slipped there was always Saturday afternoon confession. Life was very simple.

I'm sure there were many instances that began to change my mind, but the most prominent one in my recollection was in 1976, when I took the position of campus minister at Long Island University in downtown Brooklyn. An experimental program had just begun. They accepted men who were given early parole to attend classes at the university. I volunteered to work with their parole officer, offering any support I could to the men in the program. On several occasions this led me to court when one of the men slipped back and once again was in violation of the law. I would spend days sitting and waiting for court proceedings. I sat for hours outside the courtroom waiting and listening as they told stories of their childhood, their experiences, and what life up to that point had been like. I spent many hours just listening and taking it all in.

David, one of these young men, asked me one day if I would go with him to see his grandfather who had died. I accepted the invitation and journeyed with him deep into Brooklyn. It was a neighborhood I would never in my life have seen or known existed if I had not accepted his invitation. We traveled on a subway train that consisted, as I remember it, of only two cars. I was the only white person aboard and was viewed with suspicion.

When we reached our destination, I found myself in the middle of what appeared to be a bombed-out city. My thoughts turned to a poster I had seen of Archbishop Dom Hélder Câmara of Recife, Brazil, who had recently visited the United States. Under his photo, taken in a place similar to the place where I was standing, were his words, "Excuse me, America." Here I was in this place hidden from most Americans, looking for a funeral home to pay my respects to a man I had never met. I was accompanying his grandson who wanted to say goodbye.

We had to knock on the locked door of the funeral home. The man who answered the door told us they were held up at gunpoint the night before and robbed. I saw a man in a coffin in a room near the door, and presumed this was David's grandfather. I was wrong. The man who had opened the door for us opened a closet and rolled out the grandfather of this young man. He did not have a room, a place for his grandfather, but was kept in the closet until this moment when his grandson asked to see him and to say goodbye.

Love had led us to this place where, even in death, poverty had robbed this man of dignity. Love had led me to this place of truth I never would have known had I stayed in my protected world. I knew that my father would have cringed to know that I was in this place of danger. And I understood. If I had known the extent of danger in going to this place, perhaps I wouldn't have gone. But somehow now that I was there I did not experience a feeling of danger, only one of revelation. How far into the truth did I want to go? All the way in would involve a good deal of letting go.

This and many other stories can tell you the tale of how my mind was changed. The sides were disappearing, breaking down. This path that I was on was leading to a place where there were no sides, only connection and communion.

My father and I talked about my changing mind, and why I went to jail. He was helped along in understanding my actions by two archbishops: Raymond Hunthausen, the archbishop of Seattle, who testified at my trial, and Archbishop Óscar Romero, who had been assassinated in El Salvador. When Archbishop Hunthausen took the witness stand at my trial to testify to the rightness of my actions, I think it helped my father to accept my breaking of the law. My father needed that reassurance.

My father and I went together to see the film *Romero*. I knew it would help him to understand why I had been arrested in a congressional office on Long Island soon after the murder of six Jesuit priests by the military of El Salvador. The U.S. Congress had just approved millions more dollars of aid to El Salvador. Being the good and compassionate man I knew my father to be, he left the theater convinced that I had been right in doing what I did. Our minds were being changed. Óscar Romero risked death by telling the truth, and in that risk-taking, he helped to change my father's mind and mine.

Telling the truth as you know it often causes division. Love, listening, and dialogue heal and lead to understanding.

• 25 •

How Maps Connected Me to Grief and Meaning

My relative Jonas is a young man now.[1] I have been making monthly dates with him since he was eight. When I was younger and able to walk long distances, we hiked to beaches on Long Island and to other places of interest. One of his favorite places to visit is the motherhouse of the Sisters of St. Dominic. There he has met many elder sisters who have come to the motherhouse after years of service in various ministries. They have now in a sense come home to where they started, to find the rest and help they need for their aging and in most cases their ailing bodies. Their spirits are alive and active. It's their muscles and bones and sometimes their minds that have weakened and show signs of aging.

Jonas is on the autism spectrum and has difficulty focusing his attention. He sometimes goes off into fantasy and needs to be called back to the real. At times his anxiety gets the better of him and he melts down. Jonas was adopted from South Korea when he was five months old. His parents were not aware at the time of Jonas's autism, but they have loved and cared for him

---

1. His name has been changed to preserve his privacy. Although his mother granted permission for me to share his story, he is not able to consent, so I gave him a different name and am deliberately unclear about the family relationship.

and taught him to accept himself, to strive for all that he can be, to care about and love others, and to trust and have faith in God.

Something beautiful happened when the sisters at the motherhouse and Jonas met. At the heart of their relationship was an acceptance by each of the fragility of the other. They were not there to do a project or accomplish anything, but just to be together and enjoy that time. Jonas always seems to be without any anxiety around these elder sisters. I think he knows intuitively that he can be himself, and he will be accepted and loved. I believe that many of the sisters feel the same.

Our monthly outings have been a gift to me in many ways. I remember especially one of those days when we spent time together. Jonas loves to be around water. It seems to focus and relax him. The same is true about reading maps. He loves to read them, and he can spend hours at a time uninterrupted . . . just him and the maps.

On one of our outings we went to Barnes & Noble to spend some time before going out to one of Jonas's favorite restaurants. I knew that Jonas would love to be among the maps, and I could sit nearby reading, a favorite pastime of mine. I had brought no book, though, so when passing a table of new arrivals of books about Earth and things related to ecology and our present situation, I stopped to take a look. Among all the books displayed, one was prominent in getting my attention. It was titled *The End of Ice*. Its author was Dahr Jamail. I took a seat with direct vision to Jonas's activity and began to read this book. Its subtitle read, *Bearing Witness and Finding Meaning in the Path of Climate Disruption*.[2] At the time, I was immersed in the data surrounding the climate crisis and was imagining the future we were leaving for the children, all the species that were already going extinct, and the loss of biodiversity and beauty. I found

---

2. Dahr Jamail, *The End of Ice: Bearing Witness and Finding Meaning in the Path of Climate Disruption* (New York: New Press, 2019).

it incomprehensible that we could be destroying our home, this beautiful planet Earth. I knew the grief and the losses. I had a sense that there was nothing I could really do to stop climate disruption and all the destruction and loss of life that was coming in its path. The book I now held in my hands was intriguing. Finding meaning amid all the destruction was certainly something I was looking for.

My time with Jonas had led me to a place of discovery. I became immersed in the book; Jonas immersed in the maps. I read a good deal of the book during our time at Barnes & Noble. I know it will be on the list of books that have been of great influence in the way I think about life and the times we are living through. I bought the book, of course, and have returned to it many times. It is a permanent fixture on my bookshelf. Just imagining the truth of the end of ice and what that means is enough to spend a lifetime comprehending. But more than that it is the message of grieving, and how important grief is to our global life now.

I have been touched and inspired by the work and writings of Joanna Macy since the early eighties. She has related to many groups through the years. I first became a follower when she did the work of dealing with the grief we hold as children of the nuclear age. I was no stranger to the importance of being in touch with grief. But Dahr Jamail's book somehow brought some new learning to me. I had not until now thought of the connection of grief with meaning in one's life. This book helped me understand that I can bring meaning to all the destruction, all the loss, through grieving.

When we really love, we grieve the loss of the one we love. We need to fall in love with Earth and be with her as she loses all she loves. We need to be with her as she experiences the dying happening all around her.

We need to be totally present as we would a dying friend. *The End of Ice* touched a place in me that knew the truth Jamail spoke, and the love he had for mountains that had been in his life for so long. Now the ice was melting. The life on the mountain and his life were in mourning together. They were one. His presence was what he wanted to give to Earth. There are many lessons in this book that deserve the time to speak and learn about. For now I focus on the grief, and how the grief can be a gift that leads us deeper into love and to becoming the humans we are meant to be. This is something we all can do together to make a difference and discover meaning. Rather than deny the truth we see before our very eyes and become numb, or worse yet, cynical, we can grieve together and become more alive with passion, depth, and love for all that gives life meaning.

It is not money, success, and fame that give life meaning. Shopping does not do the trick. We have known that for a long time. In our time, although it seems so strange to say, perhaps it is grief that gives life meaning. This is a surprising truth but one that we can see makes sense. When all that is beautiful and life-giving is being lost, what else would there be to do but grieve? Could it be that this is the action we are called to in order to evolve and lay foundation for a new world to be born, a world born from grief because we loved so deeply? I do not mean we sit and grieve all day, although there might be many days and weeks where we do just that. But there is so much more to do, and grief might lead us to a deeper place and knowledge of a gift that only we can give. The world is desperately in need of beauty and creativity. Regeneration is still possible. Imagination can lead us to surprising things. The Universe is no stranger to death. As we look back on the story of how all things came to be, we see that death is necessary in order to bring forth new life.

Love leads to grief. Who knows where grief will lead us? Perhaps it will connect us to the truth of who we are, each one of us, and that special gift that only we can give.

My time with Jonas at Barnes & Noble brought a great learning to my life. Who knows why reading maps brings more peace to him, more focus? While he was engrossed in geography, I found my footing and was grounded in a truth and was surprised. I had found a place to stand. Jonas and I, it seems, had both been involved in contemplating geography. How far in do you want to go? The question was still drawing me further and further into the truth.

As I write this in August 2021, the United States withdrew from Afghanistan a few days previously. The weeks before were filled with pictures and experiences that were hard to take in. Desperation, compassion, anger, and rage—all the emotions you could imagine—filled our days. Marines holding weapons, and also holding children. It was a background and a reality that consumed the hours of our days as we tried to go on with life. Along with rage and anger there was blame, lots of it, and vows of revenge. The president promised, supposedly in the name of all of us, "We will not forgive. We will not forget. We will hunt you down, and make you pay."[3]

It seems the war making and the reality of "collateral damage," which translates often into the lives of children, will continue. And I am left to wonder, if we could replace blame and revenge with grief, would a different future emerge?

In the case of climate disruption, biodiversity loss, and all the realities that lead to the end of everything, there is no central figure to blame. It is all of us, culprits all. Where would we focus our revenge? Like Afghanistan, there is failure to live with—failure on an immense scale—and grief. I wonder if this unexpected path is the way leading us home.

---

3. Joseph R. Biden Jr., "Remarks by President Biden on the Terror Attack at Hamid Karzai International Airport," August 26, 2021. Available in full text at www.whitehouse.gov.

• 26 •

Joy in Grief

How do we live in joy in a climate-crisis world when we know what's up ahead? How do we live in paradise when we have made such a hell of things?

If we are not living in denial these questions arise. They are the challenging questions of our times. How do we live full of passion and love, and know that life is good? How do we not give up on life and belief in the future when we see destruction and collapse all around us?

Stories have energy. They capture moments in the past and move us forward into new action. When we are connected to the Story of the Universe, a whole new world opens up for us. We come to know that we are the Universe thinking, creating, dying, and leaving, arriving and striving, expanding, exploding into new life, dreaming always to lift the veil and know that all is one. We live in communion with all that is different and beautiful, and this gives meaning and purpose to our lives. It is possible to live in paradise even now amid the suffering and loss, the breaking down, the breaking open into new pathways, new forms, new ways of being.

And we tell stories as we cry and laugh and yearn so deeply for the truth. I am the Universe conscious. I live in awe and wonder at the beauty of it all and accept the pain and suffering that somehow is an essential part of paradise, and necessary for becoming even more than I could ever understand. Perhaps this is the mystery with which we live.

Is embracing grief the way into an unknown future? Grief is the only response when all you love is being destroyed and lost and it seems there is nothing you can do. Could this be the answer? Could grief somehow be the way to evolve into who we are meant to be? Could grief lead us to new life, a life where all of us are valued and respected, even the smallest of creatures?

I never planned for the day I would drive from coast to coast, from east to west to meet the Trident submarine and say no. I never could have dreamed I'd have the energy or guts. It seems, looking back, like I was carried there, moved by unseen energy and driven by a passion I had never known before. I met and joined others who were so moved to come together and say no to this abomination and yes to life. It was our own stories (or were they our own?) that brought us to this place of action.

I never dreamed when answering a call to leave the world I knew and enter a community of women vowed to contemplation and action that one day I would set my sights on farming, though I had no knowledge or expertise or even the equipment to succeed at such a task. And yet today I look out over ten acres that has been saved in perpetuity for the growing of food and the gathering of a community of people and plants, bees and ants, earthworms and ladybugs. It is a miracle not of my own making, but of an energy within us that, when responded to, creates more than we could have ever expected. It is the power of the Universe.

It seems looking back that my story was and is connected to other stories: to Franz Jägerstätter and Martin Luther King; to Gandhi, Jesus, and Jim and Shelley Douglass; to Bob Aldridge, Thomas Berry, Brian Swimme, and Miriam McGillis; to Joanna Macy and Dahr Jamail; to John Lewis, Raymond Hunthausen, and Óscar Romero; to Julian of Norwich and Hildegard of Bingen; to Thomas Merton and Pierre Teilhard de Chardin.

We are all united in the Story of the Universe, in the story of stars and galaxies, of bacteria and worms, the story of fish and of the osprey, the story of the wolf and the maple tree. We all come from the same origin story. So many tales in the past and trillions more to come, all connecting and moving in the direction of life.

How awesome to be a part of it all in this moment! Paradise!

But this does not remove me from suffering and grief. I still think of the children, and how they will suffer in the future as Earth becomes so hot, and life and beauty diminish even more. I've tried to do my little part in preparing them by helping them to love Earth and see the worms and bees, the microbes and all of life as part of the community, and know themselves not as consumers but as stardust.

When I went out into the Strait of Juan de Fuca on the West Coast of the United States to say no to Trident and yes to life, it did not matter if my action did not stop the submarine from deployment. When I attempted to put myself between a train carrying nuclear weapons and the Trident submarine, again to stand on the side of life, I knew the train would probably still come, again and again. The thing that mattered most of all was saying no to a world of separation, and of power over, a world of cruelty, and saying yes to life, to oneness and compassion, to love.

That train still runs through our lives. It is the train of putting money and power over life, the train of disconnection from Earth and her wisdom. I think of Daniel now and the picture of that little child I carried with me onto the tracks. "His name is Daniel, and he's asking us to stop the train," I said to anyone within hearing distance. The children and the flowers, the young of every species are asking us to stop the train so that they might live. We may in the long run not be able to stop the destruction of life that seems to be bringing us to the edge of extinction, but our lives will have purpose and meaning if we raise our voices and take action over and over again in the name of life.

Let's love Earth together. Let's grieve and suffer with her. Let's celebrate, dance, sing, and love one another as we grieve.

Let's be alive and filled with passion as we live, knowing the pain that's up ahead and the challenges that are so overwhelming.

We are the Universe conscious of itself, with powers we have never known. There is so much more to discover by going through the reality that is now before us. Let us not deny reality and truth in order to avoid the pain.

Let's embrace our times with all the unknown and know that there is one sure thing: we are going home together. Let's know real liberation. Let's go all the way in.

• 27 •

Thich Nhat Hanh

Thich Nhat Hanh, known by his students and those close to him as Thay ("teacher" in Vietnamese), died—or as his Buddhist community would say, he began his journey of transitioning—on January 22, 2022, just as I was finishing writing this book. I had often heard him say in many of his teaching sessions, "There is no birth; there is no death. There is only continuing life." So I understood how and why his Buddhist community was relating to what Christians would call his death.

I considered Thay my teacher, although I never met him one on one, only in a group. He had been a mentor since my years as a newly vowed Dominican sister, and I have gone back again and again to try to live the mindfulness he knew and practiced. For many years I've kept a new calendar on the wall beside my desk with his words, as a reminder to live the truths he taught.

Like the Trappist monk Thomas Merton, I found myself loving and seeing such truth in Buddhism as I listened to Thay's teaching. I knew it was not calling me away from my Christian beliefs, but uniting with and deepening them. I also know that through deep listening, attention, and concentration, he experienced what scientists are now discovering—that we are one and connected to everything. He was the epitome of non-dualistic thinking, and he knew that what we call good and bad live within each of us. In his poem "Please Call Me by My True Names" he wrote:

I am the child in Uganda, all skin and bones,
my legs as thin as bamboo sticks.
And I am the arms merchant,
selling deadly weapons to Uganda.

I am the twelve-year-old girl,
refugee on a small boat,
who throws herself into the ocean
after being raped by a sea pirate.
And I am the pirate,
my heart not yet capable
of seeing and loving.[1]

This kind of knowing the oneness of us all leads to such compassion and peace, such understanding and love.

I remember during my years at Ground Zero learning this lesson from Jim and Shelley Douglass. The Trident submarine that can destroy life on Earth is our own ego written large. The Trident exists outside of us because it is first inside of us. And like Thay, we can say, "I am the one resisting and saying no to Trident," and also, "I am the captain and the crew." This way of seeing changes everything. It removes separation and judgment, calls us to accountability, and makes a way for communion.

It was on June 13, 1982, that I had the chance to be in the same room as Thich Nhat Hanh, to be physically present with him for the first time. On that day I had joined millions of people on the streets of New York to call for the elimination of nuclear weapons. I had been informed that he would speak at the chapel

---

1. Thich Nhat Hanh, "Please Call Me by My True Names," in *Call Me by My True Names: The Collected Poems of Thich Nhat Hanh* (Berkeley, CA: Parallax Press, 1999), 72–73. Full text of the poem is available at the Plum Village website, https://plumvillage.org/articles/please-call-me-by-my-true-names-song-poem.

across the street from the United Nations. I had been in that chapel before and knew that it was small and could not hold a large crowd. I was determined to be present, and went early to secure my place.

The chapel was full to capacity when the time came for Thay to arrive. As he walked in, holding a beautiful red rose, I was struck by his small stature. The first thing I heard him say in his very quiet voice was to ask if anyone had a child with them. A woman holding a toddler came forth. The child who had been a bit fussy began to look at Thay holding the vibrant flower. The entire room went silent as this small child and Thay looked into each other's eyes. Time seemed to stand still. I don't know how many minutes passed when we all heard the message Thay had come to bring.

"If we could look like this into the eyes of every child in the world, there would be peace."

He had not delivered a long speech or even a teaching with many words. But I will never forget the message I heard that day.

The *New York Times* reported on this historic day in New York City. They said it was probably the largest demonstration in the history of New York. The *Times* reported a response from a man in the crowd who had driven overnight for the event: "There's no way the leaders can ignore this now. It's not just hippies and crazies anymore. It's everybody."[2] But that man and many of us who believed the government could not ignore us were wrong. They have.

Forty years have passed since that historic march in New York City, my hometown. We've made some progress. The Treaty on the Prohibition of Nuclear Weapons (TPNW) is now part of international law. It is a legally binding instrument that bans nuclear weapons. As of now none of the nuclear-armed states

---

2. Paul L. Montgomery, "Throngs Fill Manhattan to Protest Nuclear Weapons," *The New York Times*, June 13, 1982, A1.

have signed the treaty. It gives us yet another chance to pressure them, especially those that call themselves democracies, to listen to the people and obey the law.

But perhaps we all need to go deeper than laws and demonstrations. I believe we need to listen to Thich Nhat Hanh and the message he delivered in the UN chapel forty years ago. We need to look into one another's eyes and really see.

Thich Nhat Hanh was transitioning on January 22, 2022, as the James Webb telescope was making its journey to its home in space. It arrived on January 25, four days before Thay's funeral. It will be the instrument through which we learn more about the Universe and ourselves. Thay didn't need to journey home. He always knew he was already there. He tried to teach us that. When we take each step in mindful walking, we remember we have already arrived.

We are already home.

Good Friday (1999)

I didn't go to stations of the cross today
I sat beside the Long Island Sound
Present
Good Friday
Suffering crucifixion

I thought of Millstone and all the places
Dealing death to water
Source of life
I wept for future generations
Remembering another Sound
West Coast Puget Sound and Trident submarine

The bombs drop today on Kosovo
I weep standing by the cross
On the way home I spot an osprey
Sign to me that we can change
I pick up daffodils
And carry them home
Reminder of spring promise

• 28 •

No Final Chapter

There really is no final chapter concluding my storytelling. I wrote in Chapter 1 that I wanted to begin with "the final chapter," which was me at home at Homecoming Farm. But really there is no final chapter to the story. There is only ongoing life. My understanding of reality has shifted and changed since knowing and living within the Story of the Universe, how things emerge and change and grow, become more complex. There is no ending in the Story of the Universe, my story. Life and the stories go on. The Beloved Community, the dream of Gandhi and Martin Luther King, is still evolving. Many are adding to its reality. We are realizing we have one origin story. We all come from Earth, related no matter our color, gender, religion. The forests, rivers, the mountains, insects, and flowers, all kin. We are—as Robin Wall Kimmerer, author of *Braiding Sweetgrass*,[1] once said—"mutually relating to each other within the community of life." It is happening, contrary to TV news reports, which are blind to this reality. But we humans who have been gifted with this understanding are able to choose to live in this reality and do the work of living it. And by living it help it materialize. That is at the heart of the Great Work that Thomas Berry calls us to embrace. This to me is a sacred task, filled with joy and purpose. It is a way of going all the way in; into the truth that makes us free. It is the way of liberation. The journey we

---

1. Minneapolis: Milkweed Editions, 2013.

have made as a human species to arrive at the understanding that we are Earth and Universe conscious of itself, able to look back at our own story and know it for the first time, is an awesome reality. I am so privileged to have been born at this moment in Earth's history. Gratitude and celebration are my response.

But there are still realities that need ending: racism, gender inequality, hatred of the other, war.

We are in the middle of a war of terror as I write in early 2022. The people of Ukraine are fleeing as refugees of war while their loved ones remain to defend their homes, their land. The world is watching a terrible crime being committed, and we are told that the only way of ending this crime is to provide more and more weapons. We are taught to believe that the one with the most weapons wins. But there really are no winners. The weapons are the instruments of the destruction. Everything is being targeted: the buildings, the children, the aged, the streams and rivers, the trees and plants, the soil, all of life. The weapons are the instruments of death; the crimes of war belong to all of us. We are seeing its results each night on our televisions. We frame it as the good overcoming evil. And certainly war crimes are being committed. But those crimes are deep and wide and live within a way of thinking that death and war can lead to life and justice. We need to change our minds, our way of thinking. We need to end the crime and put an end to weapons of war and the mind in us that sees them as a solution.

I heard a news report when this latest war began. A Russian soldier was overheard saying, "We don't know who to shoot. They look like us."

We could stop the shooting, stop the war, if we could just see that everyone is us.

• 29 •

One More Story

Please allow me to tell you one more story. Without this story you would not be reading this book. There would be no book.

In October 2019 I learned about a conference taking place at Georgetown University, "Thomas Berry and *The Great Work*." Thomas was a person who had so much influence not just on my life but on the creation of Homecoming Farm. I wanted to be at this conference with others who shared my love for Thomas and were involved in doing what he called "The Great Work," which is in his words, "To carry out the transition from a period of human devastation of the Earth to a period when humans would be present to the planet in a mutually beneficial manner."[1]

Jayne Anne McPartlin, who was a shareholder in our organic farm, also had a deep love for Thomas and wanted to accompany me to the conference. Because I had limited funds and the cost of hotels close to Georgetown in Washington, DC, was very expensive, we set out to find a way to be able to attend. We knew that Mary Evelyn Tucker was to be a speaker at the event, and I contacted her to ask if she might know of some cheaper accommodations. That was the beginning of this beautiful story that created the book you are about to finish.

Mary Evelyn led us to a small house within walking distance of the university. There we met Professor Carole Sargent, a

---

1. Thomas Berry, *The Great Work: Our Way into the Future* (New York: Harmony/Bell Tower, 1999), 3.

woman with a vision and a very large heart who was just beginning to establish an interfaith community for global scholars in
Georgetown for short research visits. She also welcomed people
in religious life who were either doing research at the Jesuit university or there for conferences and symposia. This "beehive"
house grew out of her two-plus years living with the Society of
the Sacred Heart (RSCJ), and helping them open Anne Montgomery House, a faith-based peace community near Catholic
University. For a few days, Jayne Anne and I found a home in
DC, a place that welcomed and nourished us as we attempted
to grow in the understanding of what it meant to do "The Great
Work."

Within just hours of arriving and getting settled, I saw a photo
on a bookshelf in the living room of this home. It was a beautiful
photo of Sister Anne Montgomery, who was now deceased, but
whom I came to know through a passion we both shared in life:
to put an end to the Trident submarine and a world with nuclear
weapons. When I met Anne she had a history of resistance to
the Trident in Groton, Connecticut, where it was made. I was
resisting at its final destination, the Bangor Submarine Base on
the Kitsap Peninsula in the state of Washington. And so I asked
Carole, "I see you know Sister Anne Montgomery?" She didn't
meet Anne before she died, but she did know her protégée, Sister
Megan Rice, who joined us that evening. Then I began to tell
them the story of how I was connected to Anne, and this led to
other stories.

Carole asked me the next morning at breakfast if I would
consider allowing her to record my stories. And that was the
beginning of a journey together through stories that began to
live again, to be remembered and spoken. I believe telling the
stories created the space for a new reality in a relationship that
was forming between Carole's life and mine. We were involved
not just in a task but in a new creation.

I spent a year and a half meeting with Carole on Zoom every

Wednesday afternoon, just telling one story after another. We wondered together where this was all leading, but we let go of any expectations and were happy to just allow the stories to lead us, I realize now, to create a new way of writing a book based in relationship. After all, this is the kind of Earth and Universe we are living in, where everything is in relationship to everything else. There is no such thing as doing something alone or being a self-made person. We are made up of relationships. I found this experience of telling the stories in relationship to Carole and her life, her vision, her experiences to be a way of revelation and emergence. I felt connected to the process of the Earth and Universe in the very telling of the stories. And in the end, although I did the writing, this book emerged as a gift.

But that's not the end of the story. Another character and relationship entered halfway through, when Carole asked me if she could invite her filmmaker friend, Tim Casey, to join us on Wednesday afternoons for an hour on Zoom. Tim saw the possibility of making a film in the telling of the stories. He became another person involved in the writing of this book as we met for yet another year or more, with the stories as our connecting link. It is amazing to me how a relationship developed between me and Tim, a man I have never met face to face, who lives thousands of miles away on the West Coast of the country. It helped me see how wonderful technology made by human hands can be such a source of discovery and creativity if used in a way leading to goodness and life. What some see as the dreaded Zoom calls and meetings was for me an instrument of connection and creativity. I learned a lot about Tim Casey, his life and work, his deep commitment to silence and meditation—the source, I'm sure, of his creative work. I felt gifted by his presence and his encouragement as the pages of this book were born.

I cannot end the story of the writing of this book without including all the people at the Deeptime Network, who gather together with the leadership of Jenifer Morgan and Stephan

Martin to create new realities out of the understanding that we are all the Universe conscious of itself with awesome powers to create a world of mutuality and celebration.

I was taking one of the courses offered by the Deeptime Network while at the same time meeting with Carole Sargent and Tim Casey. I therefore was meeting each week again on Zoom with people from all parts of the country and world; people from Australia, the Philippines, Mexico, and China, people from the east and west and middle of America. We all were connecting out of a deep desire to live the New Story of the Universe and be part of creating a new consciousness where all of us humans and more than humans were living in mutuality within the community of life. This connection that I felt with all of these people and with the rivers and mountains, all the creatures and especially with a relationship that deepened between myself and the Great South Bay here on Long Island held within it for me the energy I needed to believe that I could be the author of this book.

It is with deep gratitude that I tell this story of the writing of this book and all the members of the community of life who helped me express new insights and understandings leading me deeper into the truth and true liberation. I thank Jim Douglass for that question heard so many years ago: "Just how far would you like to go in?"

I invite all of us to treasure the stories of our life and to get to know the Story of the Universe, which beckons all of us to go all the way in.

Afterword

So many of the Ground Zero newsletters surfaced from my files as I was writing this book. I share here a paragraph from a beautiful article written about community by Shelley Douglass in the November/December issue of 1984. Shelley titled the article "Seeing the Invisible" and ended it with the sentence, "Community is the invisible truth of our oneness becoming visible in our lives." Here is a paragraph that stood out to me in the article:

> We live and think communally because we are already part of the deep and profound community of creation. The reality that underlies our existence is a communal one, this earth is a community of beings, a harmonious unity which lives and grows and suffers and dies during every moment of every day, each single being affecting the other one. Community is not something we build, it is something we uncover. It is a fact of life. We are one.[1]

It seems to me that our times are calling us to uncover and live this truth today as violence and inhumanity escalate and bring us to the brink of extinction.

We need to journey into the New Story, the Story of the Universe.

Thomas Berry's teachings have changed my life and given me a gift so precious that words cannot accurately convey the depth of meaning that gift brings. Communion and belonging come to mind.

---

1. Shelley Douglass, "Seeing the Invisible," *Ground Zero Newsletter*, Ground Zero Center for Nonviolent Action, November/December 1984.

We have been given community.

As I sit beside the Great South Bay here on Long Island, the watershed of Homecoming Farm, I have been given the capacity to intimately know this beautifully flowing body of water; to know it as myself embedded in a community of life wide and alive with stars and galaxies. Beneath the Bay is a community of life I cannot see, but I feel its presence. The sun lovingly gives away her energy and life, the wind whips up waves, the seagulls play above. War's destruction and inhumanity enter in; my grief present, holding me close. But knowing and experiencing this community of life brings messages of faith and trust in transformation.

And I hear Thomas's voice in the waves. *Tell them the story.*

Homecoming is not far off. It's already here in seed.

The spiritual journey is a journey home to the true self. We are on this journey together. That self is bigger, wider, deeper than anything we've ever known.

Gratitude

Impressions on a rock
How many years it takes
Of wind, sand, sea and storm
To form it into something new.
To wear away and leave a scar
Or on the other hand to make of it
A masterpiece of beauty.

Not half as long for human heart and mind
Three years, or months, or weeks
The time is unimportant.
The scars are there detracting
From a beauty that might have been.

But deeper than the scars
That cut and wear away
Are other imprints.
These add the color, fullness, beauty
To my being.
Unlike the rock, I can be grateful
For having been impressed.

Stay

This poem was written at Crystal Spring, an ecological learning center where I spent every Holy Week from the middle to late nineties with women trying to live the New Story. It was a special place, a special time.

Stay, stay, stay
And wait, wait, wait in the present moment
I want to move, to do, to change things
Take control.
But I must stay and wait
Nailed to the present moment.
To the place of tension where action seems fruitless
And inaction no choice at all.
Stay, wait there
Stay on the shifting cracking moving ground
Transporting me to where I need to go.

No answers
No goals or direction
No solution to the devastation done by human hands
Surrender
Find the courage to surrender
To grieve the passing and the death
The birds still sing
The sun still shines

The water still flows to the sea
Crow builds nest

Will love prevail amidst the loss and grief?
Stay, stay, stay
Love, love, love
Love deeply in the staying.

Litany to Mary

When I came to know the trees and rivers and all of creation as my sisters and brothers, my community, the litany to Mary opens out and becomes more inclusive.

Mother of the trees and rivers
Mother of the earthworms
Mirror of the rocks and mountains
Model of our inner space
Keeper of our dreams and visions
Mother bursting from the fire
Virgin centered in the Universe
Virgin flowing with the streams
Virgin whispering with the wind
Virgin dark and deep and rooted
Mother of the soils and shells
Mother colored by the Earth
Mother burning with the story
Pregnant one, creative fire
Mother of the Universe
Mother of our heart's desire

Christmas Letter

December 24, 2020

Dear Family & Friends,

The words we are hearing along with the Christmas music this year are, "Stay home."

For those of us privileged enough to have a home with heat and food, the request seems like a fairly easy one with which to comply, especially when its purpose is to try to slow down a deadly virus and help in the long run to save lives. Of course we will miss the gatherings and celebrations with family and friends, especially with the ones we haven't seen in a while. Staying home seems so ordinary. It doesn't seem like Christmas.

The pandemic is with us this Christmas asking us to stay put, slow down, open up to the messages and the many truths we might have missed if things had stayed "normal."

I am in touch on Zoom with people from many parts of the world who are trying to find ways to create a new normal with more inclusion, connection, justice, compassion, and, most of all, love. Christmas at home, perhaps with less noise, fewer distractions might give us a chance to listen to what Christmas is all about. It might help us to delve deeper and find a meaning that has escaped us in our consumer-oriented world.

I'm sure that all of you have thoughts and feelings on all that has happened to us in the last ten months or so. It would be wonderful to have a gathering to talk about the meaning of it all and where we might be being led. For now I'm staying home; I'm trying to listen.

Meister Eckhart, a Dominican, born in the late thirteenth century, has given us words that lead to the real meaning of Christmas. "We are all meant to be mothers of God; for God is always in need of being born." This time of pandemic, of darkness, not knowing the future can lead us to a new place, a place of birth. The divine and human are not separate, but one. We have the power to give birth to God; to be the light in the darkness. All it takes is to really believe in Christmas.

Love,
Jeanne

"Let us believe in the New Year; new, untouched, full of things that have never been."

Rainer Maria Rilke

Good Friday by the Water

We put God to death each day
In many ways destroying life
Take power and crucify the innocent
In El Salvador, Iraq, Afghanistan

We have forgotten we are one body
We destroy ourselves.

So many ways to kill the living God
Dealing death to Rainforest and Redwoods
Oceans, sounds and rivers
Birds who songs are stilled
While we build places to buy and sell
No lasting song for soul and heart

We have forgotten we are one body
We destroy ourselves

So many ways to kill the living God
Forgive us

We know not what we do
But if we know we grieve
We cannot stand the pain
At the cross we mourn
While God is crucified

We ask for wisdom and for strength
To change ourselves
To see
To know the oneness of it all
To speak and be the truth
To stop the crucifixion
The slaughter of the living God.

Short Poems

Blue-green planet Earth
Faithfully circling the sun
You are my body.

You are grandmother
Tiny rocks by seashore found
Grey, blue, pink, orange.

Spider spinning webs
Teach me what I need to know
Tell me your secret.

Earth Madonna calls
Her blackness teaches something
Moist and dark the Earth.

Seed tiny treasure
Reaching for the light of love
Dies and is reborn.

Fire inside me
Burning with many colors
Source of all that is.

The soil brings forth fruit
A transubstantiation
Apple becomes me.

Red-winged blackbird sing
Tell me of my island home
Stay with me awhile.

When the winter ends
I sit and await with joy
Friend osprey's return.

To Learn More

To learn more about Thomas Berry, Brian Swimme, and the Story of the Universe, see the following resources.

Berry, Thomas. *The Dream of the Earth* (San Francisco: Sierra Club Books, 1988).

————. *The Great Work: Our Way into the Future* (New York: Harmony/Bell Tower, 1999).

Morgan, Jennifer. *The Universe Story Trilogy* (*Born with a Bang, From Lava to Life, Mammals Who Morph*) (Naperville, IL: Dawn Publications, 2002). For ages 8 through adult.

Swimme, Brian. *The Universe Is a Green Dragon: A Cosmic Creation Story* (New York: Bear & Company, 1984).

————. *The Hidden Heart of the Cosmos: Humanity and the New Story* (Maryknoll, NY: Orbis Books, 1996).

Swimme, Brian, and Mary Evelyn Tucker. *Journey of the Universe* (New Haven, CT: Yale University Press, 2014).

Tucker, Mary Evelyn, and John Grim. *Thomas Berry: Selected Writings on the Earth Community* (Maryknoll, NY: Orbis Books, 2014).

Websites

Carole Sargent's interfaith community: www.publishing advising.com/house

Deeptime Network: dtnetwork.org

Ground Zero Center for Nonviolent Action, gzcenter.org

Homecoming Farm: www.homecomingearth.org

Pax Christi, www.paxchristiusa.org

Thomas Berry, official website: thomasberry.org

Tim Casey's filmmaking. To learn more about Tim Casey's filmmaking you can find him at "Timothy O. Casey" on the
Internet Movie Database (www.imdb.com).

World Beyond War, worldbeyondwar.org

Yale Forum on Religion and Ecology: fore.yale.edu

Acknowledgments

My gratitude to Carole Sargent and Tim Casey, who gave so much of their time, energy, and love to the pages of this book. To Jim and Shelley Douglass, Marya Barr, Karol Schulkin, Rene Krisko, Jim Jarosz, Maggie Kirry, and George and Linda Greenwald, who made up the Ground Zero community in which I was challenged to know and live the truth of nonviolence. And to Bill and Kim Wahl and all the folks in Seattle who joined us in joyful resistance to the Trident submarine. You remain a part of the great story we told with our lives. To Glen Milner and Mary Gleysteen, who along with others continue the work of Ground Zero alongside the Trident submarine base. To Robert and Janet Aldridge, whose courage to leave Lockheed Martin in fidelity to truth planted the seeds, producing hundreds of actions to resist the Trident submarine.

To Bishop Thomas Gumbleton, whom I joined at the Nevada Nuclear Test Site, where he risked arrest and walked behind a banner that stated, "The Church Is Crossing the Line." And to Bishop Raymond Hunthausen, who crossed another line in not paying taxes for weapons and war, and who named the Trident "The Auschwitz of Puget Sound." To Bishop Óscar Romero, who gave his life for telling the truth about the oppression of the people in El Salvador. These bishops inspired and challenged me. They gave me hope. To Franz Jägerstätter, who refused to fight in Hitler's army, and whose dream about the train going to hell led me to Ground Zero.

To Thomas Merton, whose contemplative spirit rooted in everyday life attracted me since novitiate days, and to Thich Nhat Hanh, who challenged me to pay attention and live each moment. For Daniel Berrigan, who first led me into resistance, and to all those who continue to say No to death and Yes to life. To Agnes Kelly and all the folks of Pax Christi Long Island who continue to give a voice to a nonviolent way of living. To Carol Feeney, whose love and creativity helped me fall in love with Nashville, Tennessee, and learn lessons I am still unpacking from my time when it was home to me. To all my Dominican Sisters who supported me along the way, even when they did not understand where I was going, and for their generosity in providing the land now called Homecoming Farm.

To my Mom and Dad and my fun-loving family, whose love and loyalty have always surrounded me and helped me to continue to be me. To Miriam McGillis, who led me to the deep and transformative teachings of Thomas Berry, and for Brian Swimme, who through science brought the New Story alive for me. For Mary Evelyn Tucker, who along with Brian Swimme created the film *Journey of the Universe*, and for Mary Evelyn's encouragement as I put the final touches on this book. For the Elderberries, a group of elder women who have remained faithful to the study of the teachings of Thomas Berry and have been such a nourishing presence in my life. For Jennifer Morgan, Stephan Martin, and all the folks at the Deeptime Network who surrounded me with imagination, creativity, and a commitment to keep finding ways to live and communicate the New Story.

To my dear friend Chris Loughlin OP, with whom I learned the Story and found ways to make it real in my life. To Carolyn McDade and Joyce Rouse, whose music I have shared with countless people along the way and which continues to lift my spirit. To Yanira Chacon, Gladys Murillo, and Cecelia Moran, who opened up a whole new world for me as they brought their gifts and their beautiful country of El Salvador and its people into my life. It was the Salvadoran people who led me back to the land.

To Florence Kissane and Karen Oxholm, who opened their homes to me and gave me space to explore the east end of Long

Island and come to know my island home in surprising and beautiful ways. For Tom Stock and Sister Joyce Hummel, who experimented and created with me new ways of teaching children to love Earth and know the story of the sun, water, planets, and creatures in the soil, all part of the community we love. For Elizabeth Keihm, who like the sun has given so much of her energy away in order to give life and nourishment so that Homecoming Farm can continue to live. For Don, our farmer, all the folks who have served on the board of Homecoming Farm through the years, the apprentices and interns, the volunteers and shareholders who helped create a community with soil, seed, and food at its center. For Christine Keihm, Father Marty Hall, and the numerous people who have shared their resources and helped us to continue telling the Story at Homecoming Farm. For Sister Eileen McCormick, who in her quiet way has supported me throughout my journey and continues to keep our books balanced at the farm. For the Eagle Scouts, their families and troops who built the infrastructure of the farm, whose energy and love will remain into the future.

For Robert Ellsberg and his team at Orbis Books who have allowed my voice to be heard and to be among so many authors I so admire.

For the bees, the ants and earthworms, the microbes in the soil, the birds, the herbs, the flowers, and all the creatures who create life and beauty and reasons to celebrate. For the Great South Bay and for the sun who gives away her energy and makes all life possible.

And to the children and the young of every species, who encourage me each day to remain faithful to life. You are all a part of the Story. This book belongs to all of you.

Index